MASTER CLUB CURRICULUM
Building Martial Arts Knowledge

This Book Belongs to:

_____

Master Club Curriculum - Martial Arts Knowledge

© 2010, 2012, 2014 by Greg Moody, KarateBuilt L.L.C. and Achievement Consulting.

All Rights Reserved.
Reproduction or translation of any part of this work beyond that permissible by section 107 or 108 of the United States Copyright Act without permission of the copyright owner is unlawful.

3rd Printing: 2014
2nd Printing: 2012
1st Printing: 2010

For information or bulk sales contact:
KarateBuilt L.L.C.
1900 W. Chandler Blvd. Ste. 15-352
Chandler AZ 85224
Corporate@KarateBuilt.com

Contents

Colored Belt Curriculum — 3
    1° Adult & Kid Black Belt Planner: — 5
    TINY TIGER 1° Black Belt Planner: — 7
  Colored Belt FORMS — 9
    Master Club Form Requirements: — 15
      Choongjung Ee-Jahng — 18
      Choongjung Il-Jahng — 21
      In Wha Ee-Jahng — 24
      In Wha Il-Jahng — 27
      Songahm Oh-Jahng — 30
      Songahm Sah-Jahng — 32
      Songahm Sahm-Jahng — 36
      Songahm Ee-Jahng — 38
      Songahm Il-Jahng — 40
  Colored Belt SELF DEFENSE — 43
    Self Defense (A) — 44
    Self Defense (B) — 45
    Self Defense (C) — 46
    Self Defense (D) — 47
    Self Defense (E) — 48
    Self Defense (F) — 49
  Colored Belt WEAPONS — 51
    Colored Belt Weapons Form Patterns - Overview — 55
    Colored Belt Jahng Bong — 61
    Colored Belt Bahng Mahng Ee Partner Drills — 65
    Colored Belt Bahng Mahng Ee Form — 67
    Colored Belt Ssahng Jeol Bong Form — 71
  Colored Belt SPARRING — 73
    Sparring Reaction Drills — 75
  Colored Belt BREAKING — 77

Black Belt Curriculum — 81
  Black Belt Uniform Requirements — 82
  Black Belt Fitness Requirements — 84
    Black Belt Fitness Requirements — 85
  Black Belt Open Hand Curriculum — 87
    Pressure Point Control Tactics (PPCT) — 89
      PPCT Flow (Outside) — 91
    Joint Locks — 93
      Joint Lock Basics (A) — 94
      Joint Locks – Flow (A) — 95
      Joint Lock Flow Drill #1 (A) — 96
      Joint Lock Basics (B) — 97
      Joint Locks – Flow (B) — 98

Joint Lock Flow Drill #2 (B)	99
Spontaneous Knife Defense System	105
Ground Fighting	109
Ground Fighting Basics (A)	110
Ground Fighting Drill (A)	111
Ground Fighting Basics (B)	112
Ground Fighting Drill (B)	113
Combatives	119
Combative Training	120
1° Black Belt Curriculum	**123**
2° Black Belt Planner:	125
Shim Jun	127
Board Break Requirements:	131
Ssahng Jeol Bong Combat Drills	133
Single Ssahng Jeol Bong Form	134
Bahng Mahng Ee Combat Drills	138
Single Bahng Mahng Ee Form	139
2°R Black Belt to 2°D Black Belt Rank Requirements:	145
2° Black Belt Curriculum	**147**
3° Black Belt Planner:	149
Jung Yul	151
Board Break Requirements:	155
2° Black Belt Decided	155
Double Ssahng Jeol Bong Drills	157
Double Ssahng Jeol Bong Form	159
Double Bahng Mahng Ee Drills	165
Double Bahng Mahng Ee Form	169
Ssahng Nat Form	175
3° Black Belt Curriculum	**181**
4° Black Belt Planner:	183
Chung San	185
Board Break Requirements:	189
3° Black Belt	189
Mid Range Jahng Bong Form	191
Jee Pahng Ee Basics	197
Jee Pahng Ee (Cane) Form	199
Long Range Jahng Bong Floor Drills	205
Long Range Jahng Bong Form	207
Sahm Dahm Bong Drills	213
Sahm Dahm Bong Form	215
Oh Sung Do (OSD) Form	221
Gumdo (Sword) Form	223
Creative Form	227
4° Black Belt Curriculum	**235**
5° Black Belt Curriculum	**257**

Leadership Training Applications   279
Supplemental Material   283

My Notes on My Road to Master

 *My Notes on My Road to Master*

Welcome to the Master Club!

Black belt is a special rank. It is a new beginning of the path toward mastery in the martial arts. You can become a master! This manual includes all of the requirements a black belt must fulfill to achieve 5th degree Black Belt. This includes weapons, joint manipulation, ground fighting, pressure point control tactics and of course traditional Songahm Taekwondo. Your instructors at the Black Belt Academy are the key to learning this material and growing in martial arts and as an individual. Ask them if you have any questions about any part of this manual. Good luck on your road to Mastery! Note: All of the material herein is subject to change and improvement. As with all curriculum, your instructor at your school will advise you on the material you will learn.

Curriculum Rotation

MASTER CLUB CURRICULUM • Building Martial Arts Knowledge

Class	January Graduation	March Graduation	May Graduation	July Graduation	September Graduation	November Graduation
Colored Form	SA2 / Basics	SA1 IW2^{even} / SA4^{odd}	SA3 / Basics	SA2 IW1^{even} / CJ2^{odd}	SA1 / Basics	SA3 SA5^{even} / CJ1^{odd}
Colored Weapon	SJB Form	JB Basics & Partner Drills	JB Form	BME Basics & Partner Drills	BME Form	SJB Basics & Tricks
Black Belt Form (Open Hand)	Joint Locks	Ground Fighting	Ground Fighting	Pressure Points	Pressure Points	Joint Locks
1° Weapon	BME Use of Weapon & Combat Drills	BME Form	SJB Use of Weapon & Combat Drills	SJB Form	Knife Defense & Use of Knife	Knife Form
2° Weapon *	1st Half Form Focus	2nd Half Form Focus	1st Half Form Focus	1st Half Form Focus	1st Half Form Focus	2nd Half Form Focus
3° Weapon **		Ssahng Nat (Double Kama)		Double SJB Form		Double BME Form
	JB Form (Mid^{even} / Long^{odd} Range)		SDB^{even} Form / JPE^{odd} Form		OSD^{even} Form / Gumdo^{odd} Form	

*2° Recommended Black Belts do the same material as 1° Black Belts. **4° and up follow special schedule (see 4° Curriculum Rotation)

Required Equipment**

Korean Name	Common Name	Abbreviation	Required
Ssahng Jeol Bong	Nunchaku	SJB	2 @ Colored Belt
Bahng Mahng Ee	Stick	BME	2 @ Colored Belt
Practice Gun	Practice Gun	Gun	Colored Belt
Jahng Bong	Staff or Bo	JB	Colored Belt
Practice Knife	Practice Knife	Knife	1°
Ssahng Nat	Double Kama	SN	2°
Jee Pahng Ee	Cane	JPE	3°
Sahm Dan Bong	3 Sectional Staff	SDB	3°
Oh Sung Do	Broadsword	OSD	3°
Gumdo	Sword	Gumdo	3°

REV 4.0 - © KarateBuilt L.L.C.

Master Club

Colored Belt Curriculum

Rev 4.0 - © KarateBuilt L.L.C.

My Notes on My Road to Master

My Road to Black Belt!

1° Adult & Kid Black Belt Planner:

Take a minute and plan your road to 1° Black Belt. Your instructor can help you find the correct dates. You should plan on graduating every 2 months.

Current Rank	Testing For:	Requirements:	Graduation Fee:**	My Test Date
White	Orange	16 Classes (2 Months) Current Curriculum and Black Belt Attitude! **Safety Weapon(s) are Required at Each Class.**	$70	__/__/__
Orange	Yellow	16 Classes (2 Months), Current Curriculum & Black Belt Attitude! **Safety Gear and Weapon is Required at Each Class.**	$75	__/__/__
Yellow	Camo	16 Classes (2 Months), Current Curriculum & Black Belt Attitude!	$75	__/__/__
Camo	Midterm	16 Classes (2 Months), Current Curriculum & Black Belt Attitude! Green Level Free Sparring	$75	__/__/__
Camo	Green	16 Classes (2 Months), Current Curriculum & Black Belt Attitude! Green Level Free Sparring	$75	__/__/__
Green	Midterm	16 Classes (2 Months), Current Curriculum & Black Belt Attitude! Purple Level Free Sparring	$75	__/__/__
Green	Purple	16 Classes (2 Months), Current Curriculum & Black Belt Attitude! Purple Level Free Sparring	$75	__/__/__
Purple	Midterm	16 Classes (2 Months), Current Curriculum & Black Belt Attitude! Blue Level Free Sparring	$75	__/__/__
Purple	Blue	16 Classes (2 Months), Current Curriculum & Black Belt Attitude! Blue Level Free Sparring	$75	__/__/__
Blue	Midterm	16 Classes (2 Months), Current Curriculum & Black Belt Attitude! Brown Level Free Sparring	$75	__/__/__
Blue	Brown	16 Classes (2 Months), Current Curriculum & Black Belt Attitude! Brown Level Free Sparring	$75	__/__/__
Brown	Midterm	16 Classes (2 Months), Current Curriculum & Black Belt Attitude! Red Level Free Sparring	$75	__/__/__
Brown	Red	16 Classes (2 Months), Current Curriculum & Black Belt Attitude! Red Level Free Sparring	$75	__/__/__
Red	Midterm	16 Classes (2 Months), Current Curriculum & Black Belt Attitude! Red Level Free Sparring	$80	__/__/__
Red	1° R	16 Classes (2 Months), Current Curriculum & Black Belt Attitude! 1°R Level Free Sparring, Fitness Test	$80	__/__/__
1° R	Midterm	16 Classes (2 Months), Current Curriculum & Black Belt Attitude! 1°R Level Free Sparring	$80	__/__/__
1° R	1° D	16 Classes (2 Months), Current Curriculum & Black Belt Attitude! 1° Level Free Sparring, Fitness Test	$80	__/__/__

* Ssahng Jeol Bong, Bahng Mahng Ees, Jahng Bong, Safety Gear and Combat Bahng Mahng Ee Required for Master Club Classes. All Requirements subject to change.
** Graduation fees and requirements subject to change.

Rev 4.0 - © KarateBuilt L.L.C.

My Notes on My Road to Master

My Road to Black Belt!

TINY TIGER 1° Black Belt Planner:

Parents! Take a minute and plan your child's road to black belt*. Your instructor can help you find the correct Graduation dates (they are listed on our Activity Board).
Your Tiny Tiger should be ready to Graduate every 2 months.

Current Rank	Testing For:	Requirements:	Graduation Fee:**	My Test Date
White	Orange	16 Classes (2 Months) **Safety Weapon is Required at Each Class**	$70	__/__/__
Orange	Tiger	16 Classes (2 Months), Curriculum & Attitude! **Safety Gear is Required!**	$70	__/__/__
Tiger	Yellow	16 Classes (2 Months), Curriculum & Attitude!	$70	__/__/__
Yellow	Cheetah	16 Classes (2 Months), Curriculum & Attitude!	$70	__/__/__
Cheetah	Camo	16 Classes (2 Months), Curriculum & Attitude!	$70	__/__/__
Camo	Lion	16 Classes (2 Months), Curriculum & Attitude!	$70	__/__/__
Lion	Midterm	16 Classes (2 Months), Curriculum & Attitude!	$70	__/__/__
Lion	Green	16 Clasttses (2 Months), Curriculum & Attitude!	$70	__/__/__
Green	Eagle	16 Classes (2 Months), Curriculum & Attitude!	$70	__/__/__
Eagle	Midterm	16 Classes (2 Months), Curriculum & Attitude!	$70	__/__/__
Eagle	Purple	16 Classes (2 Months), Curriculum & Attitude!	$70	__/__/__
Purple	Phoenix	16 Classes (2 Months), Curriculum & Attitude!	$70	__/__/__
Phoenix	Midterm	16 Classes (2 Months), Curriculum & Attitude!	$70	__/__/__
Phoenix	Blue	16 Classes (2 Months), Curriculum & Attitude!	$70	__/__/__
Blue	Dragon	16 Classes (2 Months), Curriculum & Attitude!	$75	__/__/__
Dragon	Midterm	16 Classes (2 Months), Curriculum & Attitude!	$75	__/__/__
Dragon	Brown	16 Classes (2 Months), Curriculum & Attitude!	$75	__/__/__
Brown	Double Dragon	16 Classes (2 Months), Curriculum & Attitude!	$75	__/__/__
Double Dragon	Midterm	16 Classes (2 Months), Curriculum & Attitude!	$75	__/__/__
Double Dragon	Red	16 Classes (2 Months), Curriculum & Attitude!	$75	__/__/__
Red	Midterm	16 Classes (2 Months), Curriculum & Attitude!	$80	__/__/__
Red	Triple Dragon	16 Classes (2 Months), Curriculum & Attitude!	$80	__/__/__
Triple Dragon	Midterm	16 Classes (2 Months), Curriculum	$80	__/__/__
Triple Dragon	1° Rec	16 Classes (2 Months), Curriculum Black Belt Attitude! Fitness Test	$80	__/__/__
1° Rec	Midterm	16 Classes (2 Months), Curriculum & Attitude!	$80	__/__/__
1° Rec	Quad. Dragon	16 Classes (2 Months), Current Form, Fitness Test Current Curriculum and Black Belt Attitude!	$80	__/__/__

* Tiny Tigers graduate to the Karate for Kids Classes with instructor permission. See the Karate for Kid "Road to Black Belt" for graduation requirements at that time. Ssahng Jeol Bong, Bahng Mahng Ee, Jahng Bong, Safety Gear and Combat Bahng Mahng Ee Required.
** Graduation fees and requirements subject to change

Rev 4.0 - © KarateBuilt L.L.C.

My Notes on My Road to Master

Master Club

Colored Belt FORMS

My Notes on My Road to Master

Colored Belt Requirements:

Now you are making the first step toward Black Belt! Forms are the most important part of your step. The Master Club in class forms are listed first. The lower level forms are also listed as a reference for leadership students. Karate Kids are required to perform one half of the adult form at graduation and Tiny Tigers perform all material with a leader. These forms prepare you for the next level of training, improve your physical conditioning and increase your ability to defend yourself.

Belt Meanings

Each rank has a special meaning. As we learn our new material, the belt we wear represents progress toward Black Belt, but it also symbolizes our growth as people. Here is a list of the special meanings of each belt:

Color	Meaning / Philosophy
White	"Pure and without the knowledge of Songham Taekwondo. As with the Pine Tree, the seed must now be planted and nourished to develop strong roots." *The student has no knowledge of Songahm Taekwondo and begins with a clean (pure) slate."*
Orange	"The sun is beginning to rise. As with the morning's dawn, only the beauty of the sunrise is seen rather than the immense power." *The beginner student sees the beauty of the art of Taekwondo but has not yet experienced the power of the technique"*
Yellow	"The seed is beginning to see the sunlight." *The student begins to understand the basics of Taekwondo.*
Camo	"The sapling is hidden amongst the taller pines and must fight its way upwards." *The student begins to realize his/her place in the world's largest martial art. The student must now begin to spar in order to be promoted in rank.*
Green	"The pine tree is beginning to develop and grow in strength." *The student's technique is developing power. The components of the basic techniques are beginning to work in unison.*
Purple	"Coming to the mountain. The tree is in mid-growth and now the path becomes steep." *The student has crossed over into a higher level of Songahm Taekwondo. The techniques, forms and level of sparring become more difficult, creating a "mountain" that must be overcome.*

ATA BLACK BELT ACADEMY

REV 4.0 - © KarateBuilt L.L.C.

Advanced Belts

When you advance past Purple belt, you should think about each of the past belt graduations you have completed. These meanings represent your growth through Black Belt and Master. Here is a list of the special meanings of each belt:

Color	Meaning / Philosophy
Blue	"The tree reaches for the sky toward new heights." *Having passed the mid-way point, the student focuses his/her energy upwards toward black belt.*
Brown	"The tree is firmly rooted in the earth." *At this point the student has mastered the basics and developed deep roots in Taekwondo.*
Red	"The sun is setting. The first phase of growth has been accomplished" *The first day (the period of time from White belt to Red belt) of growth is coming to an end. The physical skill has been developed but lacks control; therefore, physical and mental discipline must be achieved.*
1° Rec	"The dawn of a new day. The sun breaks through the darkness." *The previous day has ended giving way to a new dawn. The student must begin a new phase of training; that of being a black belt.*

 *My Notes on My Road to Master*

Master Club Form Requirements:

At the Master Club colored ranks, you are challenged to not only work on till Black Belt, but to improve them to a *Black Belt* level. Congratulations on setting your goal to *Black Belt* !! Keep working hard - Remember, Mastery doesn't end - it begins when you reach Black Belt!

My Notes on My Road to Master

Forms

Choongjung Ee-Jahng
(Choongjung #2)

The form is on the following pages. This will be performed at assigned Graduations. These are reprinted by permission of the American Taekwondo Association

Form Pattern

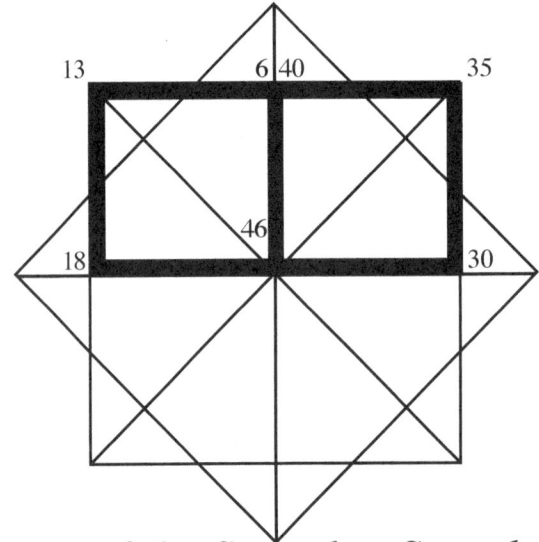

Starting at the center of the Songahm Star, the numbers represent the technique at the end of that line.

Form Segment Breakdown
2 - 4 - 4 - 4 - 4 - 5 - 4 - 4 - 4 - 5 - 3 - 3

Master Club Curriculum - Forms

Choongjung Ee-Jahng (#2)
"All Things Turn Out Perfect and Beautiful"

Technique	R/L	Stance	Section	
1. Knifehand Square Block - (Concentration - 5 Seconds)	Right	Back	High	
2. Knifehand Square Block - (Concentration - 5 Seconds)	Left	Back	High	
3. Low Block	Left	Back	Low	Line 1
4. Reverse Punch	Right	Back	Mid	
5. Low Block	Right	Back	Low	
6. Reverse Punch	Left	Back	Mid	
7. #2 Round Kick (and in a continuous motion...)	Left		Mid/High	
8. Side Kick	Left		Mid/High	
9. Double Inner Forearm Block	Left	Front	High	Line 2
10. Reverse Upset Punch (then step forward and...)	Right	Front	Mid	
11. Palm Heel Strike - **Kihap**	Right	Back	High	
12. Reverse Palm Heel Strike	Left	Back	High	
13. #2 Front Kick	Left		Mid/High	
14. Horizontal Back Elbow	Right	Middle	High	
15. Knifehand Square Block (then jump switch and land with...)	Right	Back	High	Line 3
16. Double Outer Forearm Block	Left	Back	High	
17. #3 Jump Round Kick	Left		Mid/High	
18. Double Outer Forearm Block (then right foot steps behind...)	Left	Sparring	High	
19. Double Knifehand Low Block	Right	Rear	Low	
20. Upset Ridgehand Strike	Right	Middle	Mid	Line 4
21. Reverse Hook Kick - **Kihap (End of Karate Kid Segment)**	Left		Mid/High	
22. Reverse Punch	Right	Back	Mid	
23. Ridgehand Strike	Left	Back	High	
24. #2 Round Kick (and in a continuous motion...)	Right		Mid/High	
25. Side Kick	Right		Mid/High	
26. Double Inner Forearm Block	Right	Front	High	Line 5
27. Reverse Upset Punch (then step forward and...)	Left	Front	Mid	
28. Palm Heel Strike	Left	Back	High	
28. Reverse Palm Heel Strike	Right	Back	High	
30. #2 Front Kick	Right		Mid/High	
31. Horizontal Back Elbow - **Kihap**	Left	Middle	High	
32. Knifehand Square Block (then jump switch and land with...)	Left	Back	High	Line 6
33. Double Outer Forearm Block	Right	Back	High	
34. #3 Jump Round Kick	Right		Mid/High	
35. Double Outer Forearm Block (then right foot steps behind...)	Right	Sparring	High	

Rev 4.0 - © KarateBuilt L.L.C.

Choongjung #2 - Continued
"All Things Turn Out Perfect and Beautiful"

Technique	R/L	Stance	Section	
36. Double Knifehand Low Block	Left	Rear	Low	
37. Upset Ridgehand Strike	Left	Middle	Mid	Line 7
38. Reverse Hook Kick	Right		Mid/High	
39. Reverse Punch	Left	Back	Mid	
40. Ridgehand Strike	Right	Back	High	
(then left foot steps to right, right steps back and...)				
41. Low X-Block	Both	Front	Low	
42. #2 Front Kick (landing in back)	Right		Mid/High	Line 8
43. Knifehand X-Block (then step back with left foot and...)	Both	Front	High	
44. Low X-Block	Both	Front	Low	
45. #2 Front Kick (landing in back)	Left		Mid/High	
46. Knifehand X-Block	Both	Front	High	

Choongjung Il-Jahng
(Choongjung #1)

The form is on the following pages. This will be performed at assigned Graduations. These are reprinted by permission of the American Taekwondo Association

Form Pattern

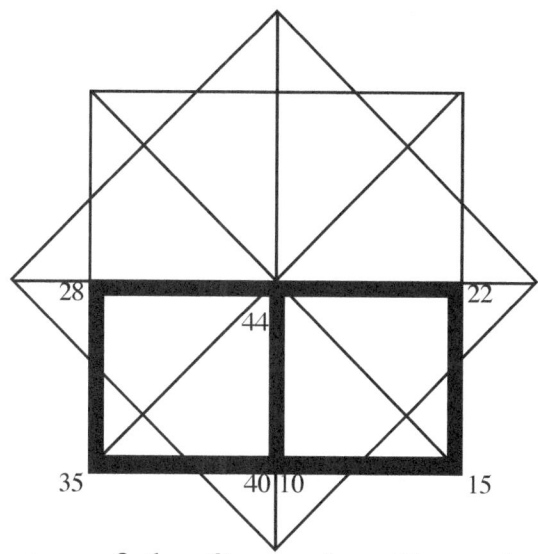

Starting at the center of the Songahm Star, the numbers represent the technique at the end of that line.

Form Segment Breakdown
3 - 3 - 4 - 5 - 4 - 3 - 6 - 4 - 3 - 5 - 4

Rev 4.0 - © KarateBuilt L.L.C.

Master Club Curriculum - Forms

Choongjung Il-Jahng (#1)
"All Things Turn Out Perfect and Beautiful"

	Technique	R/L	Stance	Section	
1.	Palm Upset Block	Left	Middle	Mid	
2.	Punch	Right	Middle	Mid	
3.	Punch (then left foot steps to right foot, right steps out...)	Left	Middle	Mid	Line 1
4.	Palm Upset Block	Right	Middle	Mid	
5.	Punch	Left	Middle	Mid	
6.	Punch	Right	Middle	Mid	
7.	(Step back with right foot...) Double Knifehand Block	Left	Back	High	
8.	Knifehand High/Low Block - (Concentration - 5 Seconds)	Right	Back	High&Low	Line 2
9.	#1 Side Kick	Right		Mid/High	
10.	Knifehand High/Low Block (then right steps to left, left out...)	Right	Back	High&Low	
11.	Reverse Punch - (Concentration - 5 Seconds)	Right	Front	Mid	
12.	#2 Front Kick - **Kihap** (and in a continuous motion...)	Right		Mid/High	
13.	Round Kick	Right		Mid/High	Line 3
14.	Double Knifehand Low Block	Right	Back	Low	
15.	Reverse Upset Knifehand Strike (front foot steps to front stance)	Left	Front	High	
16.	Upset Ridgehand Strike (back foot step to left, facing west)	Left	Rear	High	
17.	Horizontal Spearhand	Left	Back	High	
18.	#3 Jump Outer Crescent	Left		High	Line 4
19.	Reverse Palm Heel Strike	Right	Back	High	
20.	X-Block	Both	Closed	High	
21.	Knifehand Strike	Right	Closed	High	
22.	Punch - **Kihap**	Left	Closed	Mid	
23.	Double Outer Forearm Low Block	Right	Middle	Low	
24.	#1 Jump Side Kick (step together jump side kick)	Right		Mid/High	
25.	Double Outer Forearm Block (**End of Karate Kid Segment**)	Right	Sparring	High	Line 5
26.	Double Outer Forearm Low Block	Left	Middle	Low	
27.	#1 Jump Side Kick (step together jump side kick)	Left		Mid/High	
28.	Double Outer Forearm Block	Left	Sparring	High	
29.	Upset Ridgehand Strike	Right	Rear	High	
30.	Horizontal Spearhand	Right	Back	High	
31.	#3 Jump Outer Crescent	Right		High	Line 6
32.	Reverse Palm Heel Strike - **Kihap**	Left	Back	High	
33.	X-Block	Both	Closed	High	
34.	Knifehand Strike	Left	Closed	High	
35.	Punch (right foot steps 270° behind and...)	Right	Closed	Mid	

Choongjung #1 - Continued
"All Things Turn Out Perfect and Beautiful"

Technique	R/L	Stance	Section	
36. Reverse Punch - (Concentration - 5 Seconds)	Left	Front	Mid	
37. #2 Front Kick (and in a continuous motion...)	Left		Mid/High	Line 7
38. Round Kick	Left		Mid/High	
39. Double Knifehand Low Block	Left	Back	Low	
40. Reverse Upset Knifehand Strike (front foot steps to front stance)	Right	Front	High	
(then right foot steps to left, and left steps back and...)				
41. Double Knifehand Block	Right	Back	High	Line 8
42. Knifehand High/Low Block - (Concentration - 5 Seconds)	Left	Back	High&Low	
43. #1 Side Kick	Left		Mid/High	
44. Knifehand High/Low Block	Left	Back	High&Low	

Master Club Curriculum - Forms

Name: _____

Graduation Date: __/__/__

In Wha Ee-Jahng
(In Wha #2)
"An Unbroken Glory"

The form is on the following pages. This will be performed at assigned Graduations. These are reprinted by permission of the American Taekwondo Association

Form Pattern

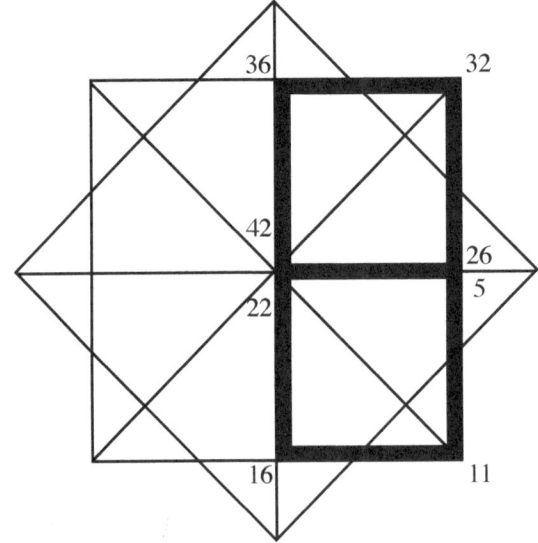

Starting at the center of the Songahm Star, the numbers represent the technique at the end of that line.

Form Segment Breakdown

5 - 6 - 5 - 6 - 4 - 6 - 4 - 6

Master Club Curriculum - Forms

Inwha Ee-Jahng (#2)
"An Unbroken Glory"

Technique	R/L	Stance	Section	
1. Right Foot Steps Right, Low X-Block	Both	Front	Low	
2. Twin Upset Punch	Both	Front	Mid	
3. Jump Front Kick (step together, jump with both legs)	Right		Mid/High	Line 1
4. Reverse Upward Elbow Strike	Left	Front	High	
5. Punch	Right	Front	High	
(then right foot half steps to left, left steps backwards and ...)				
6. Ridgehand Block	Left	Middle	High	
7. Knifehand Low Block	Left	Middle	Low	
8. #3 Hook Kick (and in a continuous motion...)	Left		Mid/High	Line 2
9. Round Kick	Left		Mid/High	
10. Backfist	Left	Middle	Mid	
11. Knifehand Strike (then right steps to left, left steps out and...)	Left	Middle	High	
12. Low X-Block	Both	Front	Low	
13. Twin Upset Punch - **Kihap**	Both	Front	Mid	
14. Jump Front Kick (step together, jump with both legs)	Left		Mid/High	Line 3
15. Reverse Upward Elbow Strike	Right	Front	High	
16. Punch (then left foot half steps to right, right steps out...)	Left	Front	High	
17. Ridgehand Block	Right	Middle	High	
18. Knifehand Low Block	Right	Closed	Low	
19. #3 Hook Kick (and in a continuous motion...)	Right		Mid/High	Line 4
20. Round Kick	Right		Mid/High	
21. Backfist	Right	Middle	Mid	
22. Knifehand Strike (then left foot steps to...)	Right	Middle	High	
23. Knifehand Low Block - **Kihap (End of Karate Kid Segment)**	Left	Closed	Low	
24. #1 Side Kick	Left		Mid/High	Line 5
25. #3 Hook Kick	Left		Mid/High	
26. Double Knifehand Block	Left	Back	High	
(then right foot steps backwards 270° and...)				
27. Knifehand Square Block	Right	Back	High	
28. Reverse Upset Knifehand Strike	Left	Back	High	
29. Punch (then right foot steps to front stance and...)	Right	Back	High	Line 6
30. Head Grab	Both	Front	High	
31. Knee Strike (then left foot lands, right steps out and...)	Left		Mid	
32. Side High/Low Block (then left foot steps to right and...)	Right	Middle	High/Low	

Rev 4.0 - © KarateBuilt L.L.C.

Inwha #2 - Continued
"An Unbroken Glory"

Technique	R/L	Stance	Section	
33. Knifehand Low Block - *Ki-hap*	Right	Center	Low	Line 7
34. #1 Side Kick	Right		Mid/High	Line 7
35. #3 Hook Kick	Right		Mid/High	Line 7
36. Double Knifehand Block	Right	Back	High	Line 7
37. (step to west...) Knifehand Square Block	Left	Back	High	Line 8
38. Reverse Upset Knifehand Strike	Right	Back	High	Line 8
39. Punch (then right foot steps to front stance and...)	Left	Back	High	Line 8
40. Head Grab	Both	Front	High	Line 8
41. Knee Strike	Right		Middle	Line 8
42. Side High/Low Block	Left	Middle	High/Low	Line 8

In Wha Il-Jahng
(In Wha #1)
"An Unbroken Glory"

The form is on the following pages. This will be performed at assigned Graduations. These are reprinted by permission of the American Taekwondo Association

Form Pattern

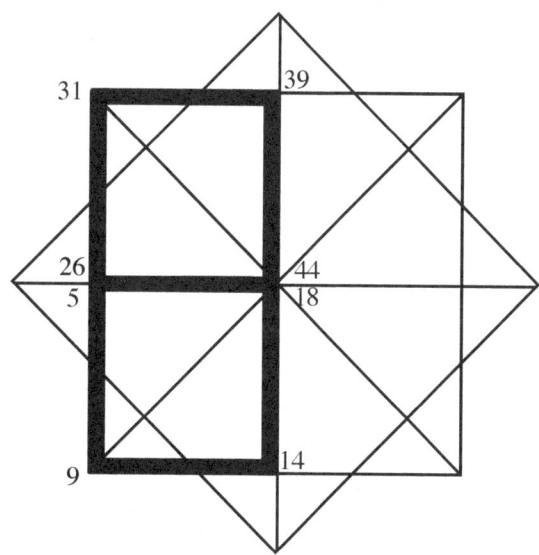

Starting at the center of the Songahm Star, the numbers represent the technique at the end of that line.

Form Segment Breakdown
5 - 4 - 5 - 4 - 7 - 6 - 7 - 6

Inwha Il-Jahng (#1)
"An Unbroken Glory"

Technique	R/L	Stance	Section	
1. Double Knifehand Block	Left	Back	High	Line 1
2. Reverse Horizontal Elbow Strike (Stepping with Front Foot)	Right	Front	Mid	
3. Inner Crescent	Right		High	
4. Reverse Side Kick	Left		Mid/High	
5. Vertical Back Elbow Strike (Hitting & Looking Behind)	Left	Back	Mid	
6. Turn to Right, Double Outer Forearm Block	Right	Sparring	High	Line 2
7. #2 (Back Leg) Round Kick (Don't Put Foot Down)	Left		Low	
8. Repeat Round Kick	Left		High	
9. Double Outer Forearm Block	Left	Sparring	High	
10. Turn Backwards to Right, Double Knifehand Block	Right	Back	High	Line 3
11. Reverse Horizontal Elbow Strike (Stepping with Front Foot)	Left	Front	Mid	
12. Inner Crescent	Left		High	
13. Reverse Side Kick	Right		Mid	
14. Vertical Back Elbow Strike - Kihap!	Right	Back	Mid	
15. Turn to Right, Double Outer Forearm Block	Left	Sparring	High	Line 4
16. #2 (Back Leg) Round Kick (Don't Put Foot Down)	Right		Low	
17. Repeat Round Kick	Right		High	
18. Double Outer Forearm Block (End of Karate Kid Segment)	Right	Sparring	High	
19. Turn 270° to Right, (Right Foot In Front), Square Block	Right	Back	High	Line 5
20. #2 (Back Leg) Front Kick (Don't Put Foot Down)	Left		High	
21. Side Kick, (Land in Right Front Stance)	Right		Mid	
22. Vertical Punch	Left	Front	Mid	
23. Vertical Punch	Right	Front	High	
24. Step Forward, Punch - Kihap!	Left	Back	Mid	
25. Knifehand Strike	Left	Back	High	
26. Step with Back Foot, Front High/Low Block	Right	Closed	High&Low	Line 6
27. Step to Back (On High Side), Double Knifehand Block	Left	Back	High	
28. Spearhand	Right	Back	High	
29. Front Leg Outer Crescent to Left Target	Left		Mid	
30. Single Knifehand Outer Forearm Block	Right	Middle	High	
31. Punch	Left	Middle	Mid	

Inwha #1 - Continued
"An Unbroken Glory"

Technique	R/L	Stance	Section	
32. Step toward Punch, Square Block	Left	Back	High	
33. #2 (Back Leg) Front Kick (Don't Put Foot Down)	Right		High	
34. Side Kick, (Land in Left Front Stance) - Kihap!	Right		Mid	
35. Vertical Punch	Right	Back	Mid	Line 7
36. Vertical Punch	Left	Front	High	
37. Step Forward, Punch	Right	Front	Mid	
38. Knifehand Strike	Right	Back	High	
39. Step with Back (Left) Foot, Front High/Low Block	Left	Closed	High&Low	
40. Step Back(Left Foot "High Side"), Double Knifehand Block	Right	Back	High	
41. Spearhand	Left	Back	High	Line 8
42. Front Leg Outer Crescent to Right Target (to Middle Stance)	Right		Mid	
43. Single Knifehand Outer Forearm Block	Left	Middle	High	
44. Punch	Right	Middle	Middle	

Songahm Oh-Jahng (Songahm #5)
"Pine Tree and Rock"

The form is on the following pages. This will be performed at assigned Graduations. These are reprinted by permission of the American Taekwondo Association

Form Pattern

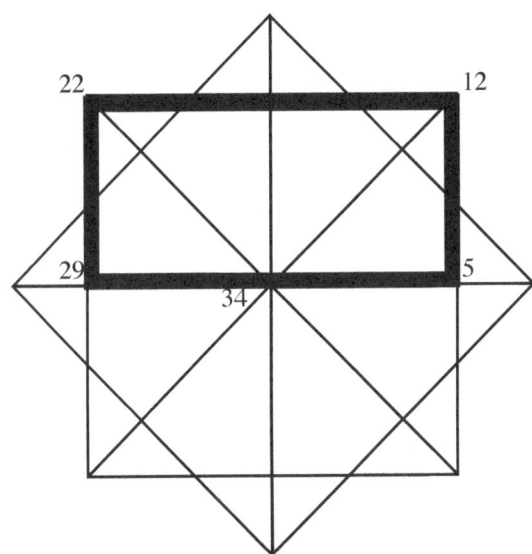

Starting at the center of the Songahm Star, the numbers represent the technique at the end of that line.

Form Segment Breakdown

5 - 4 - 3 - 5 - 5 - 4 - 3 - 5

Songahm Oh-Jahng (#5)
"Pine Tree and Rock"

Technique	R/L	Stance	Section	
1. Twin Outer Forearm Block (Stepping to Right Front Stance)	Both	Front	High	Line 1
2. #2 (Back Leg) Front Kick	Left		Mid	
3. Reverse Ridgehand Strike	Right	Front	High	
4. #1 Round Kick	Left		Mid	
5. Double Knifehand Block	Left	Back	High	
6. Pivot on Front Foot, Turn Around (270°), Outer Forearm Blk	Right	Front	High	Line 2
7. Low Block	Right	Front	Low	
8. Step to Middle Stance with Front Foot, Punch	Right	Middle	High	
9. Inner Forearm Block (Muscle Block)	Right	Middle	High	
10. #3 (Step Together) Side Kick (Land in Middle Stance)-Kihap!	Right		Mid	
11. Twin Low Block	Both	Middle	Low	
12. Twin Inner Forearm Block (Twin Muscle Block)	Both	Middle	High	
13. Step Forward (Left Foot), Double Outer Forearm Block	Left	Sparring	High	Line 3
14. #1 (Front Leg) Front Kick	Left		Mid	
15. Reverse Punch	Right	Sparring	High	
16. Step Forward, Reverse Side Kick	Left		Mid	
17. Double Outer Forearm Block (End of Karate Kid Segment)	Left	Sparring	High	
18. Twin Outer Forearm Block (Stepping to Left Front Stance)	Both	Front	High	Line 4
19. #2 (Back Leg) Front Kick	Right		Mid	
20. Reverse Ridgehand Strike	Left	Front	High	
21. #1 Round Kick	Right		Mid	
22. Double Knifehand Block	Right	Back	High	
23. Step Forward, Knifehand High Block	Left	Front	High	Line 5
24. Knifehand Low Block	Left	Front	Low	
25. Spearhand- Kihap!!	Right	Front	Mid	
26. Step to Middle Stance, Double Knifehand Block	Left	Middle	High	
27. #3 (Step Together) Side Kick (Land in Middle Stance)	Left		Mid	
28. Twin Low Block	Both	Middle	Low	
29. Twin Inner Forearm Block (Twin Muscle Block)	Both	Middle	High	
30. Step Backwards (Right Foot), Double Outer Forearm Block	Right	Sparring	High	Line 6
31. #1 (Front Leg) Front Kick	Right		Mid	
32. Reverse Punch	Left	Sparring	High	
33. Step Forward, Reverse Side Kick	Right		Mid	
34. Double Outer Forearm Block	Right	Sparring	High	

Rev 4.0 - © KarateBuilt L.L.C.

Master Club Curriculum - Forms

Name: _____

Graduation Date: __/__/__

Songahm Sah-Jahng
(Songahm #4)
"Pine Tree and Rock"

The form is on the following pages. This will be performed at assigned Graduations. These are reprinted by permission of the American Taekwondo Association

Form Pattern

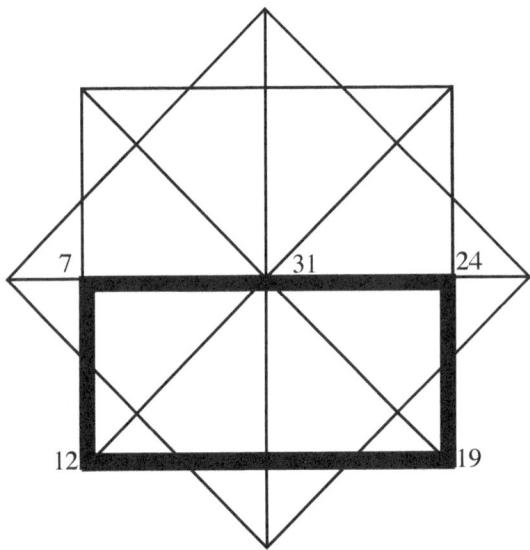

Starting at the center of the Songahm Star, the numbers represent the technique at the end of that line.

Form Segment Breakdown
3 - 4 - 5 - 4 - 3 - 5 - 4 - 3

Master Club Curriculum - Forms

Songahm Sah-Jahng (#4)
"Pine Tree and Rock"

	Technique	R/L	Stance	Section	
1.	Twin Inner Forearm Block	Both	Middle	High	
2.	Punch	Left	Middle	Mid	
3.	Punch	Right	Middle	Mid	
4.	Double Outer Forearm Block	Left	Sparring	High	Line 1
5.	#2 Round Kick	Right		Mid/High	
6.	Reverse Side Kick (Land in Middle Stance)	Left		High	
7.	Back Fist - Kihap	Left	Middle	High	
8.	Step to Right with Right Foot, Low Block	Right	Front	Low	
9.	Inner Forearm Block	Right	Front	High	
10.	Reverse Punch	Left	Front	High	Line 2
11.	#2 Side Kick (Land in Middle Stance)	Left		Mid/High	
12.	Knifehand Strike	Left	Middle	Mid	
13.	Step Right to Left, then Left out, Twin Inner Forearm Block	Both	Back	High	
14.	#3 Jump Front Kick	Left		Mid/High	
15.	#2 Front Kick	Right		Mid/High	Line 3
16.	Double Outer Forearm Block (End of Karate Kid Segment)	Right	Sparring	High	
17.	#2 Round Kick	Left		Mid/High	
18.	Reverse Side Kick (Land in Middle Stance)	Right		High	
19.	Back Fist	Right	Middle	High	
20.	Low Block	Left	Front	Low	
21.	Inner Forearm Block	Left	Front	High	Line 4
22.	Reverse Punch	Right	Front	High	
23.	#2 Side Kick	Right		Mid/High	
24.	Knifehand Strike - Kihap	Right	Middle	Mid	
25.	Step Left to Right, Right out, Twin Inner Forearm Block	Both	Back	High	
26.	#3 Jump Front Kick	Right		Mid/High	
27.	#2 Front Kick	Left		Mid/High	Line 5
28.	Double Outer Forearm Block	Left	Sparring	High	
29.	Twin Inner Forearm Block	Both	Middle	High	
30.	Punch	Right	Middle	Mid	
31.	Punch	Left	Middle	Mid	

Rev 4.0 - © KarateBuilt L.L.C.

My Notes on My Road to Master

Beginner Forms

*For reference only. This is the supplemental material for Leadership and Elite© Instructor Program students.

Beginner Forms

Name: _____
Graduation Date: __/__/__

Songahm Sahm-Jahng (Songahm #3)
"Pine Tree and Rock"

Your Rotation A form is on the following pages. Some material from this form may be performed at Graduation. These are reprinted by permission of the American Taekwondo Association

Form Pattern

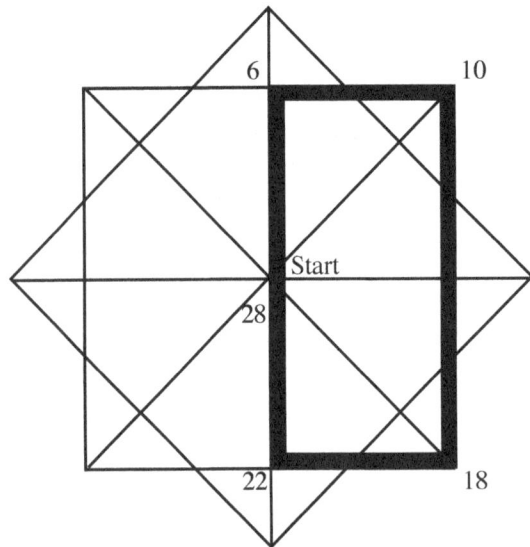

Starting at the center of the Songahm Star, the numbers represent the technique at the end of that line.

Form Segment Breakdown
2 - 4 - 4 - 4 - 4 - 4 - 2 - 4

Beginner Forms

Songahm #3
Songahm Sahm-Jahng "Pine Tree and Rock"

Technique	Side	Stance	Section
1. Knifehand Strike	Left	Back	Mid
2. Double Knifehand Block	Left	Back	High
3. #4 Front Kick (Step back with front foot first)	Right		Mid
4. #2 (Back Leg) Round Kick	Left		Mid
5. Knifehand Low Block	Left	Front	Low
6. Knifehand High Block (then right foot steps and...)	Left	Front	High
7. Punch - **Kihap**	Right	Middle	Mid
8. Punch - **Kihap** (then left foot steps backwards and...)	Left	Middle	Mid
9. Vertical Spearhand	Right	Middle	Mid
10. Vertical Spearhand	Left	Middle	Mid
11. Step Forward (Right Foot), Low Block	Right	Front	Low
12. Reverse Punch	Left	Front	Mid
13. #3 Jump Front Kick (Kicking with Front Leg)	Right		Mid
14. Reverse Punch (**End of Karate Kid Segment**)	Left	Front	Mid
15. Step Forward (Left Foot), Low Block	Left	Front	Low
16. Reverse Punch	Right	Front	Mid
17. #3 Jump Front Kick (Left Leg) - **Kihap**	Left		Mid
18. Reverse Punch (then right foot steps and...)	Right	Front	Mid
19. Knifehand Strike	Right	Middle	Mid
20. Backfist (then left foot steps backward 180° and...)	Left	Middle	Mid
21. Knifehand Strike	Left	Middle	Mid
22. Backfist (then step forward with right foot and...)	Right	Middle	Mid
23. Knifehand Strike	Right	Back	Mid
24. Double Knifehand Block	Right	Back	High
25. #4 Front Kick (Step back with front foot first)	Left		Mid
26. #2 (Back Leg) Round Kick	Right		Mid
27. Knifehand Low Block	Right	Front	Low
28. Knifehand High Block	Right	Front	High

Rev 4.0 - © KarateBuilt L.L.C.

Beginner Forms

Name: _____

Graduation Date: __/__/__

Songahm Ee-Jahng (Songahm #2)
"Pine Tree and Rock"

Your Rotation B form is on the following pages. Some material from this form may be performed at Graduation. These are reprinted by permission of the American Taekwondo Association

Form Pattern

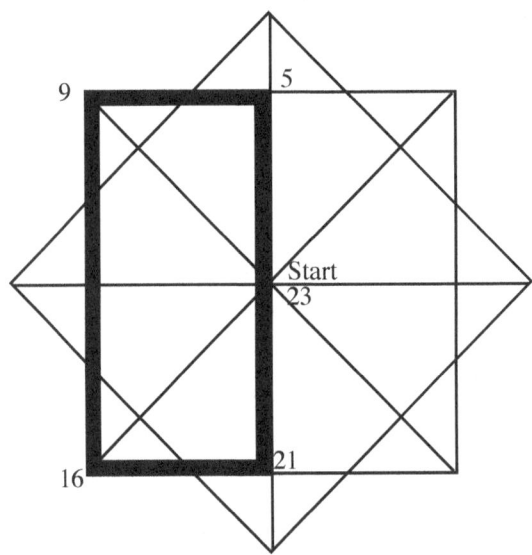

Starting at the center of the Songahm Star, the numbers represent the technique at the end of that line.

Form Segment Breakdown

3 - 2 - 2 - 2 - 5 - 2 - 2 - 2 - 3

Beginner Forms

Songahm #2
Songahm Ee-Jahng "Pine Tree and Rock"

Technique	Side	Stance	Section
1. Step Back, Double Outer Forearm Block	Left	Back	High
2. #3 Front Kick	Left		Mid/High
3. Reverse Punch	Right	Front	High
4. #2 Round Kick (land in middle stance)	Right		Mid/High
5. Twin Low Block (then left foot steps and...)	Both	Middle	Low
6. Outer Forearm Block	Left	Front	High
7. Reverse Punch (then right foot steps and...)	Right	Front	High
8. Outer Forearm Block	Right	Front	High
9. Reverse Punch	Left	Front	High
10. Knifehand Strike - **Kihap**	Left	Back	High
11. #2 Round Kick	Right		Mid/High
12. Double Outer Forearm Block	Right	Back	High
(End of Karate Kid Segment)			
13. #3 Front Kick	Right		Mid/High
14. Reverse Punch	Left	Front	High
15. #2 Round Kick (land in middle stance)	Left		Mid/High
16. Twin Low Block (then right foot steps backwards 90° and...)	Both	Middle	Low
17. Low Block	Right	Middle	Low
18. Back Fist (then left foot steps forward 180° and...)	Right	Middle	High
19. Low Block	Left	Middle	Low
20. Back Fist (then right foot steps backwards 90° and...)	Left	Middle	High
21. Knifehand Strike - **Kihap**	Right	Back	High
22. #2 Round Kick	Left		Mid/High
23. Double Outer Forearm Block	Left	Back	High

Rev 4.0 - © KaratBuilt L.L.C.

Beginner Forms

Name: _____

Graduation Date: __/__/__

Songahm Il-Jahng
(Songahm #1)
"Pine Tree and Rock"

Your Rotation C form is on the following pages. Some material from this form may be performed at Graduation. These are reprinted by permission of the American Taekwondo Association

Form Pattern

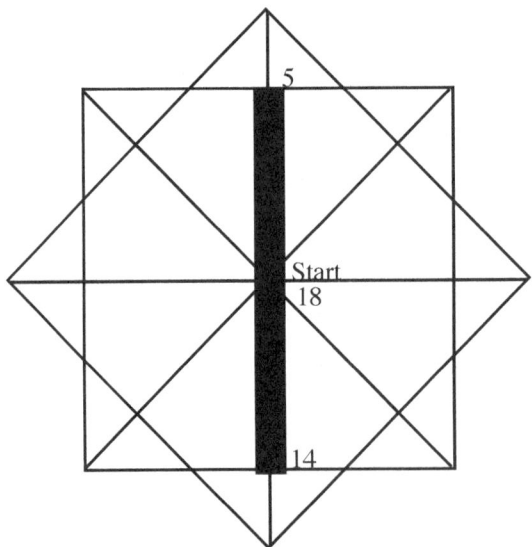

Starting at the center of the Songahm Star, the numbers represent the technique at the end of that line.

Form Segment Breakdown

2 - 2 - 2 - 3 - 2 - 2 - 2 - 3

Beginner Forms

Songahm #1
Songahm Il-Jahng "Pine Tree and Rock"

Technique	Side	Stance	Section
1. High Block	Left	Front	High
2. Reverse Punch	Right	Front	Mid
3. #2 Front Kick (land in front)	Right		Mid
4. Low Block (then left foot steps and...)	Right	Front	Low
5. Punch (then moving right foot...)	Left	Front	Mid
6. Inner Forearm Block	Right	Middle	High
7. #3 Side Kick - **Kihap**	Right		Mid
8. Knifehand Strike (then left foot steps and...)	Right	Middle	Mid
9. Punch (then right foot steps and...)	Left	Front	High
(End of Karate Kid Segment)			
10. High Block	Right	Front	High
11. Reverse Punch	Left	Front	Mid
12. #2 Front Kick (land in front)	Left		Mid
13. Low Block (then right foot steps and...)	Left	Front	Low
14. Punch (then moving left foot...)	Right	Front	Mid
15. Inner Forearm Block	Left	Middle	High
16. #3 Side Kick - **Kihap**	Left		Mid
17. Knifehand Strike (then right foot steps and...)	Left	Middle	Mid
18. Punch	Right	Front	High

Rev 4.0 - © KarateBuilt L.L.C.

My Notes on My Road to Master

Master Club

Colored Belt SELF DEFENSE

Self Defense (A)

Self Defense Number 1

Attacker: Agressive Push

Defender:

Step	Technique
1	Turn, Double Knifehand Block
2	Horizontal Elbow To Face (Repeat Elbows Until Soft)
3	Inner Crescent Kick
4	Optional: Reverse Side Kick

Self Defense Number 2

Attacker: Bear Hug

Defender:

Step	Technique
1	Side Kick (Stomp To Shin)
2	Back Elbow
3	Round Kick
4	Round Kick (Until Soft)

Note: The Self Defense letters (A, B, C, etc..) do not corespond to the rotation letter. The Self Defense that is worked on in class is based on the instructor's evaluation of student performance. Look at the Curriculum Poster for the specific defense that will be worked on in class.

MC Curriculum - Self Defense

Self Defense (B)

Self Defense Number 1

Attacker: Gun From Front

Defender:

Step	Technique
1	Deflect Gun With Left Hand (Use Webbing Of Hand), Press Gun To Attacker's Stomach And Maintain Constant Pressure
2	Palm Heel (Repeat Palm Heel Until Soft)
3	Front Kick (Optional Knee)
4	Disarm By Pulling Gun Out With Both Hands
5	Retreat With Gun Held Low

Self Defense Number 2

Attacker: Gun From Behind

Defender:

Step	Technique
1	Turn To Left, Trap Gun With Left Arm
2	Palm Heel (Repeat Palm Heel Until Soft)
3	Front Kick (Optional Knee)
4	Disarm By Stripping Gun With Right
5	Retreat With Gun Held Low

Note: The Self Defense letters (A, B, C, etc..) do not corespond to the rotation letter. The Self Defense that is worked on in class is based on the instructor's evaluation of student performance. Look at the Curriculum Poster for the specific defense that will be worked on in class.

Rev 4.0 - © KarateBuilt L.L.C.

MC Curriculum - Self Defense

Self Defense (C)

Self Defense Number 1

Attacker: Two Hand Choke From Behind

Defender:

Step	Technique
1	Turn, Twin Outer Forearm Block
2	Front Kick
3	Ridgehand
4	Push, Escape

Self Defense Number 2

Attacker: Right Punch

Defender:

Step	Technique
1	Double Outer Forearm Block
2	#1 Front Kick
3	Punch
4	Step Reverse Side Kick

Note: The Self Defense letters (A, B, C, etc..) do not corespond to the rotation letter. The Self Defense that is worked on in class is based on the instructor's evaluation of student performance. Look at the Curriculum Poster for the specific defense that will be worked on in class.

Self Defense (D)

Self Defense Number 1

Attacker: Grab From Side

Defender:

Step	Technique
1	Step into Middle Stance, Upward Palm Heel (Optional Lunch Money Peel)
2	Punch
3	Punch
4	Push, Escape

Self Defense Number 2

Attacker: One Hand Choke From Front

Defender:

Step	Technique
1	Pluck, Palm Heel
2	X-Block (Wedge)
3	Knifehand Strike
4	Punch

Note: The Self Defense letters (A, B, C, etc..) do not corespond to the rotation letter. The Self Defense that is worked on in class is based on the instructor's evaluation of student performance. Look at the Curriculum Poster for the specific defense that will be worked on in class.

Rev 4.0 - © KarateBuilt L.L.C.

Self Defense (E)

Self Defense Number 1

Attacker: Wrist Grab

Defender:

Step	Technique
1	Low X-Block (Stripping Hand Off)
2	Twin Upset Punch
3	Jump Front Kick
4	Push, Escape

Self Defense Number 2

Attacker: Knife Attack - Line 1

Defender:

Step	Technique
1	Block Knife And Upward Elbow Strike (Repeat Targeting Bicep/Radial Nerve. Chin)
2	Strip Knife

Note: The Self Defense letters (A, B, C, etc..) do not corespond to the rotation letter. The Self Defense that is worked on in class is based on the instructor's evaluation of student performance. Look at the Curriculum Poster for the specific defense that will be worked on in class.

Self Defense (F)

Self Defense Number 1

Attacker: Two Hand Choke From Front

Defender:

Step	Technique
1	Twin Inner Forearm Block (Optional Twin Pluck)
2	Punch
3	Punch
4	Push, Escape

Self Defense Number 2

Attacker: Knife From Behind

Defender:

Step	Technique
1	Grab Arm And Knife Blade (To Protect Throat)
2	Step Under Arm
3	Side Kick
4	Strip Knife

Note: The Self Defense letters (A, B, C, etc..) do not corespond to the rotation letter. The Self Defense that is worked on in class is based on the instructor's evaluation of student performance. Look at the Curriculum Poster for the specific defense that will be worked on in class.

My Notes on My Road to Master

Master Club

Colored Belt
WEAPONS

ProTech Weapons Training

ProTech is the ATA weapons, and advanced martial arts training system. These are your Graduation Requirements at the Color Belt level. As a Master Club Student, you will learn the weapons forms in class. Through this you will develop coordination, self-control, focus, and discipline. See the Black Belt Planner for graduation requirements. Students are not allowed to "play" with their weapons anywhere, and should only use them at our school under the supervision of an instructor, or at their home with the permission of their parents, practicing only what they learn in class. You must also use ATA/ProTech approved weapons, as others will not allow you to train safely. Weapons training will prepare you for *Mastery* in the Martial Arts and in life!

Name: _____

Graduation Date: __/__/__

Colored Belt Weapons Training:

Colored Belt Weapon Basics, Drills Forms are on the following pages. These are designed to train students in the weapon, and as a starting point for a competitive weapons form for Colored Belt Freestyle competition.

The Rotation for Colored Belt Weapons Training is as follows:

Rotation A - Jahng Bong Form (JB)

Rotation B - Bahng Mahng Ee (BME) Basics & Partner Drills

Rotation C - Bahng Mahng Ee (BME) Form

Rotation D - Ssahng Jeol Bong (SJB) Basics & Tricks

Rotation E - Ssahng Jeol Bong (SJB) Form

Rotation F - Jahng Bong (JB) Basics & Partner Drills

Master Club Curriculum - Weapons

Nine Lines of Attack

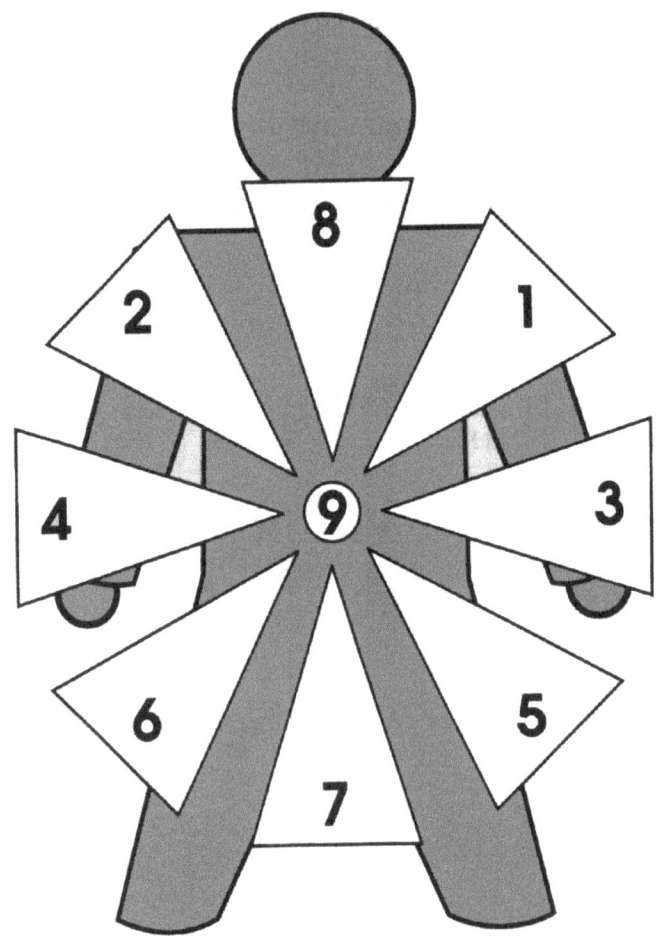

The nine lines of attack apply to all weapons and attacks. This chart should be referenced for Ssahng Jeol Bong, Bahng Mahng Ee, Jahng Bong and Jee Pahng Ee. Knife Defense has six lines of attack with 5 the same as this line 9 (there are two line 5's, line 5 low to the stomach, line 5 high to chest), and line 6 is the same as this line 8. Note: This chart shows right hand attacks - left hand attacks are a mirror image.

Colored Belt Weapons Form Patterns - Overview

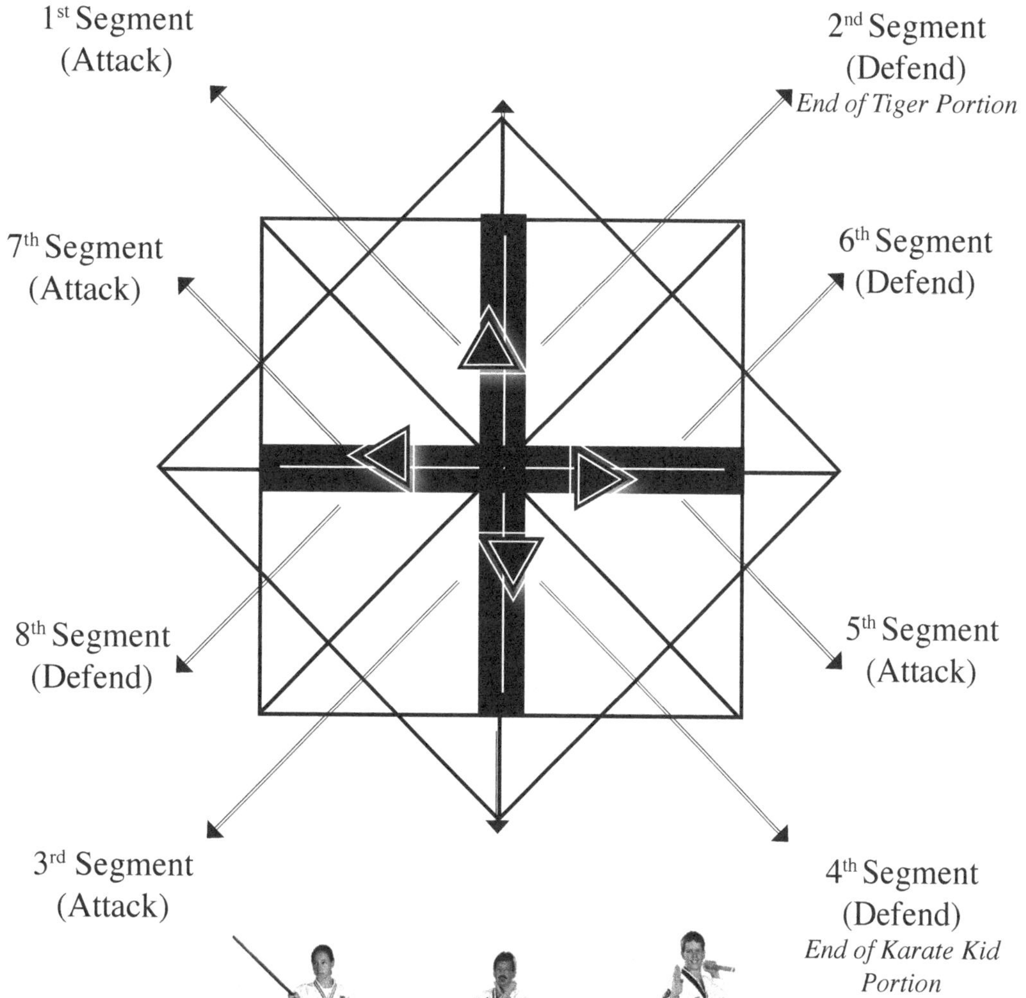

1st Segment (Attack)

2nd Segment (Defend)
End of Tiger Portion

7th Segment (Attack)

6th Segment (Defend)

8th Segment (Defend)

5th Segment (Attack)

3rd Segment (Attack)

4th Segment (Defend)
End of Karate Kid Portion

All forms start and end at the center of the Songahm Star.

My Notes on My Road to Master

ProTech Weapons Jahng Bong

The Jahng Bong (also know as the *Long Staff* or *Bo Staff*) is a weapon originated in some stories from the pole that monks in China used to carry buckets of water. When a robber would try to attack the monk, they would use these for defense.

The earliest form of the Jahng Bong, has been used throughout Asia since the beginning of recorded history.[4] The first were called (in Japan) ishibo, and were made of stone. These were hard to make and were often unreliable. These were also extremely heavy. The konsaibo was a very distant variant of the kanabo. They were made wood studded with iron. These were still too cumbersome for actual combat, so they were later replaced by unmodified hardwood staffs.

There are stick fighting techniques native to just about every country on every continent.

Master Club Curriculum - JB^mid Basics

Jahng Bong Basics - Midrange

#1 - Waist
Holding JB horizontally on right side (palm up), slide JB to left side and slide back.

#2 - Trigger Drill
Holding JB horizontally with right hand between index and middle fingers ("tiger claw grip"), bring left hand (palm up as in a knifehand) up behind the right hand. Raise JB up with "tiger claw" right hand and between thumb and forefinger of left hand. Spin down to left side with right index ("trigger") finger holding. Cross to right side and repeat.

#3 - Trigger Drill with Grab
Same start as #2, Spin JB clockwise with left hand into right hand grab.

#4 - Trigger Helicopter
Same start as #3 except: after grab with right hand, spin JB horizontally on open left palm. Then grab JB with left hand, bring down to left side, slide to right side and repeat.

#5 - Forearm Trap
Holding JB with right hand (palm up), bring JB across under left arm and rotate it clockwise over left forearm. Drop right hand and bring top of right forearm across and trap JB between forearms. Raise JB with right forearm and grab with left hand.

#6 - Backhand Roll
Holding JB with both hands palm up, left hand rolls over to thumb down/fingers up, right hand rolling over left hand. Grab with left hand. Repeat.

#7 - Palm Roll
Holding JB with right hand (palm down), spin clockwise into upward palm of left hand. Repeat.

#8 - Palm Roll and Throw
Palm roll, toss with right hand, catch with left hand.

#9 - Toe Toss
JB on ground, toe roll up to air, catch.

#10 - Helicopter
Holding JB to right side with "tiger claw" hand position, spin JB overhead, then spin over back while leaning forward.

#11 - Standing Helicopter
Holding JB with left hand (life an outer forearm block), spin the JB down and behind your back; grab it with your right hand and spin it up to over your head; grab with the left hand and repeat.

#12 - Oops Drill
Drop JB to the ground so it bounces back up - catch the other end.

Jahng Bong Twirling Drills

#1 - "V" Thumb

#2 - Double Thumb

#3 - Cross "X"

#4 - Palm Roll Over

#5 - Double Palm Up - Figure "8"

#6 - Waist Level Palm Exchange

#7 - Behind the Neck Palm Exchange

#8 - Over the Shoulder Palm Exchange

#9 - Behind the Back Palm Exchange

Master Club Curriculum - JB^{mid} Drills

Jahng Bong Partner Drills - Level 1
(Note that all of these drills and strikes must be adjusted to compensate for the attacking angle.)

Line #1 Strike
Block; strike JB; #8 strike down on hands, #1 or #2 strike on head / shoulder; #9 thrust.

Line #2 Strike
Block; strike JB; #8 strike down on hands, #1 or #2 strike on head / shoulder; #9 thrust.

Line #3 Strike
Block to side; rake hands; #8 strike down on hands, #1 or #2 strike on head / shoulder; #9 thrust.

Line #4 Strike
Block to side; rake hands; #8 strike down on hands, #1 or #2 strike on head / shoulder; #9 thrust.

Line #5 Strike
Block; strike JB; #8 strike down on hands, #1 or #2 strike on head / shoulder; #9 thrust.

Line #6 Strike
Block; strike JB; #8 strike down on hands, #1 or #2 strike on head / shoulder; #9 thrust.

Line #7 Strike
Block with JB horizontal to ground; #8 strike down on hands, #1 or #2 strike on head / shoulder; #9 thrust.

Line #8 Strike
Block with JB above head, horizontal to ground; #8 strike down on hands, #1 or #2 strike on head / shoulder; #9 thrust.

Line #9 Strike
Block and sweep to side; rake hands; #8 strike down on hands, #1 or #2 strike on head / shoulder; #9 thrust.

Master Club Curriculum - JB^mid Form

Colored Belt Jahng Bong (Mid-Range) Form

Form Pattern

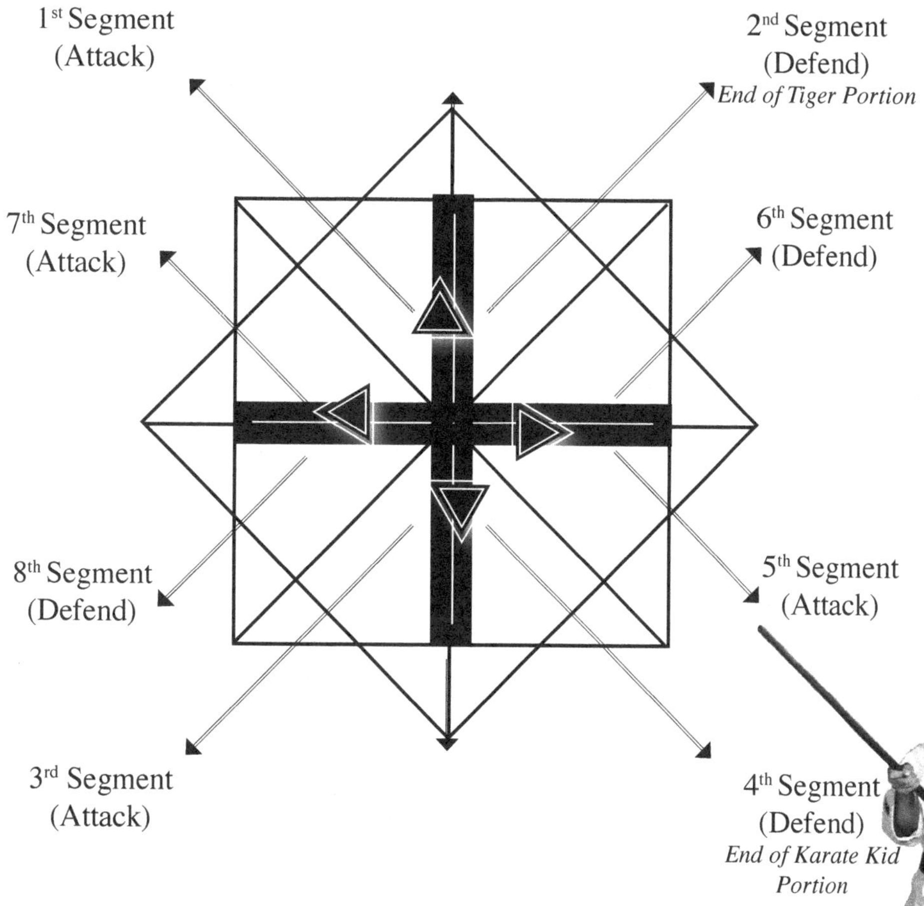

1st Segment (Attack)
2nd Segment (Defend) — *End of Tiger Portion*
7th Segment (Attack)
6th Segment (Defend)
8th Segment (Defend)
5th Segment (Attack)
3rd Segment (Attack)
4th Segment (Defend) — *End of Karate Kid Portion*

Starting at the center of the Songahm Star, the numbers represent the technique at the end of that line.

Colored Belt Jahng Bong (Mid-Range) Form

Charyut Closed Stance, JB At Right Side Held Thumbs Up.
Ready Step Right Foot To Parallel Stance, Spin JB To Left Hand, JB Held Horizontally In Front (Should Be In Over/Under Grip)

Move	Technique
1	Right Foot Steps Forward (East) To Fighting Stance, Line 1 Strike
2	Line 6 Strike
3	Circle To Right Side Line 7 Strike
4	Turn To West (Simple Turn, Feet Just Shift), Line 1 Block
5	Line 6 Block
6	Downward Line 7 Block – **Kihap** (*End of Tiny Tiger Portion*)
7	Step Right Foot To West, Crossover Line 4
8	"Cross Back" Line 3 Strike
9	Figure 8 With Right Hand
10	Turn To East (Simple Turn, Feet Just Shift), Line 4 Block
11	Line 3 Block
12	Figure 8 With Right Hand To Behind Back – **Kihap** (*End of Karate Kid Portion*)
13	Step Right Foot To Right (South), Backhand Roll
14	Line 2 Strike
15	Line 5 Strike
16	Turn To North (Simple Turn, Feet Just Shift), Palm Roll
17	Line 2 Block
18	Line 5 Block
19	Step Right Foot Forward To North, Line 8 Strike
20	Line 9 Strike
21	Helicopter
22	Turn To South, Line 8 Block
23	Line 9 Block To Right
24	Eagle Wing To Behind Back (@ Diagonal) – **Kihap**

Bahroh Step Right Foot To Parallel Stance, Spin JB To Left Hand, JB Held Horizontally In Front
Charyut JB to Right Side Held Thumbs Up as Right Foot Steps To Closed Stance

Note: These can be done as partner drills - Attack 1 vs Defense 1

ProTech Weapons Bahng Mahng Ee

The Bahng Mahng Ee (also know as the *Single Stick*) is based on a fighting systems have strong historical roots from Indonesian martial arts that are Chinese influenced.

Other systems that have similar movements to many Filipino systems also find their roots from Ch'uan Fa. There are even counts of lost Ch'uan and Tai Chi double stick forms that many of the fleeing renegade monks would have trained for in that period.

Single Bahng Mahng Ee Basics
Basics (Line 1, 2, 3)

Basic	Description
1	1, 2, 3 Angles of Strikes
2	Basic Blocks of 1, 2, 3
3	Odd Line "Snake" Disarm
4	Even Line Disarm
5	Disarms Without BME
6	Horizontal Fan Strike
7	Vertical Fan Strike

Basics (Line 4, 5, 6)

Basic	Description
1	4, 5, 6 Angles of Strikes
2	Basic Blocks of 4, 5, 6
3	Odd Line "Snake" Disarm
4	Even Line Disarm
5	Disarms Without BME
6	Forward Twirl
7	Reverse Twirl

Basics (Line 7, 8, 9)

Basic	Description
1	7, 8, 9 Angles of Strikes
2	Basic Blocks of 7, 8, 9
3	Odd Line "Snake" Disarm
4	Even Line Disarm
5	Disarms Without BME
6	Figure 8
7	Reverse Figure 8

Colored Belt Bahng Mahng Ee Partner Drills

Drills / Partner Drills

Drill 1
Line 1 Strike (Partner Also Doing Line 1)

Drill 2
Line 1 Strike + Line 6 Strike (Partner Also Doing Same)

Drill 3 (end of Tiger Portion)
Drill 2 + Line 2 Strike (Partner Also Doing Same)

Drill 4
Drill 3 + Line 5 Strike (Partner Also Doing Same)

Drill 5
Drill 4 + Line 9 Strike (Partner Also Doing Same Except Line 9 Defense Is A Downward Sweeping Block)

Drill 6 (Extra Credit)

A	B
High Block	Line 8 Strike
Line 1 Strike	Line 1 Cover Block
Line 2 Cover Block	Line 2 Strike
Line 8 Strike	High Block
Line 1 Cover Block	Line 1 Strike
Line 2 Strike	Line 2 Cover Block

Drill 10 (Extra Credit)

A	B
High Block	Line 8 Strike
Line 1 Strike	Passing Block
2 Handed Down Blk	Line 4 Strike
Line 9 Strike	Low Sweep Blk
Line 2 Cover Block	Line 2 Strike
Line 8 Strike	High Block
Passing Block	Line 1 Strike
Line 4 Strike	2 Handed Down Blk
Low Sweep Blk	Line 9 Strike
Line 2 Strike	Line 2 Cover Block

Drill Methods – All Drills Need To Be Done With These Methods...
To Mirror, On Pad, Against Partner (even Tigers),
Sword Fighting (Down floor – one on offense moving forward, one on defense moving backward, then switch)

Notes: All Drills are progressive – 1 leads to 2, etc...
Partners need to strike at targets (neck, knee, etc) not just push sticks around.

Rev 4.0 - © KarateBuilt L.L.C.

Additional Single Bahng Mahng Ee Basics

Basic	Description
1-5	#1 through #5 Partner Drills*
6	Heel Strikes
7	High Block Disarm
8	Even Line Disarm Drill "Snake"
9	Even Line Disarm Drill "Dig"
10	Odd Line Disarm Drill
11	Pass/Strike Disarm
12	Advanced 6 Count Partner Drill*
13	Advanced 8 Count Partner Drill
14	Advanced 10 Count Partner Drill*

* Shown on prior page.

Master Club Curriculum - BME Form

Colored Belt Bahng Mahng Ee Form

Form Pattern

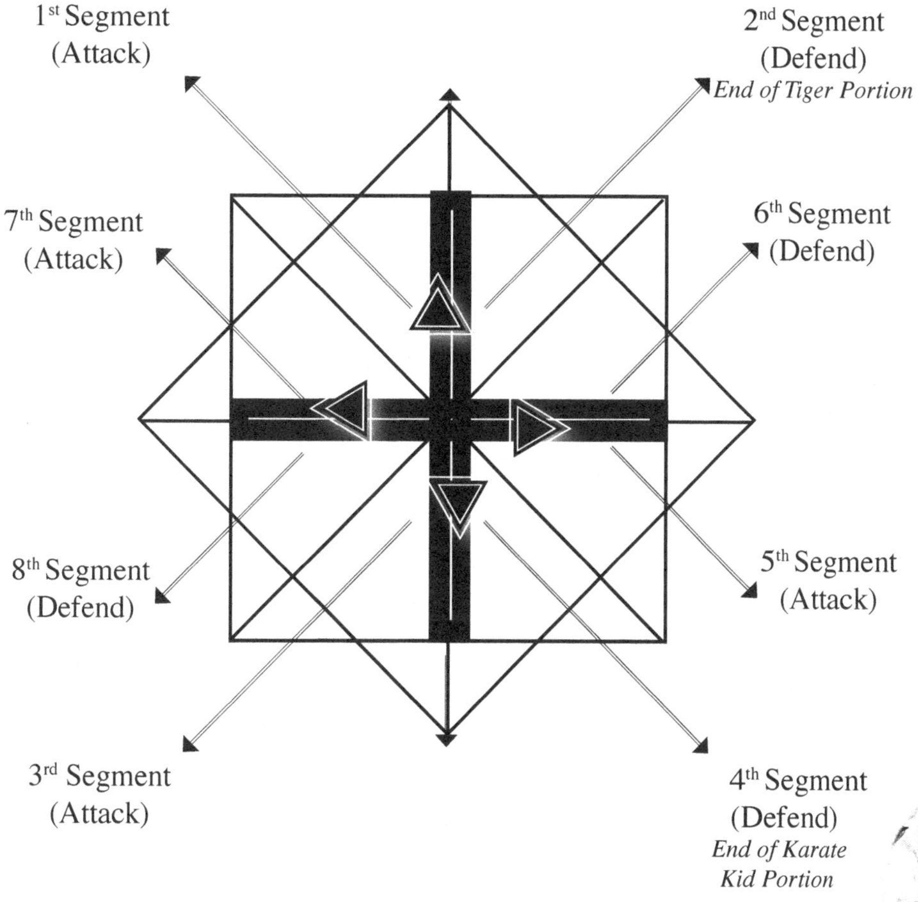

- 1st Segment (Attack)
- 2nd Segment (Defend) — *End of Tiger Portion*
- 7th Segment (Attack)
- 6th Segment (Defend)
- 8th Segment (Defend)
- 5th Segment (Attack)
- 3rd Segment (Attack)
- 4th Segment (Defend) — *End of Karate Kid Portion*

Master Club Curriculum - BME Form

Colored Belt Bahng Mahng Ee Form

Charyut Closed Stance, BME At Right Side Held Down to Side.
Ready Step Right Foot To Parallel Stance, Twirl BME, BME Held Horizontally In Front (Both Hands on Top)

Move	Technique
1	Right Foot Steps Forward (East) To Fighting Stance, Line 1 Strike
2	Line 2 Strike
3	Line 9 Strike
4	Turn To West (Simple Turn, Feet Just Shift), Line 1 Strike (as Block)
5	Line 2 Strike (as Block)
6	Downward Sweeping Block – **Kihap** (*End of Tiny Tiger Portion*)
7	Step Right Foot To West, Line 6
8	Line 3 Strike
9	Line 8 Strike
10	Turn To East (Simple Turn, Feet Just Shift), Jump Over Line 6
11	Line 3 Static Block (reinforced with hand)
12	High Block + "Snake" Disarm of Line 8 Strike – **Kihap** (*End of Kid Portion*)
13	Step Right Foot To Right (South), Line 8 Strike
14	Cover Block Line 1
15	Line 2 Strike
16	Turn To North (Simple Turn, Feet Just Shift), High Block
17	Line 1 Strike
18	Cover Block Line 2
19	Step Right Foot Forward To North, Line 4 Strike
20	Circle Line 7 Strike
21	Twirl Line 2 Strike
22	Turn To South, Static Line 4 Block (reinforced with hand)
23	Static Line 7 Block (reinforced with hand)
24	"Even" Line Disarm to a Line 2 Strike – **Kihap**

Bahroh Step Right Foot To Parallel Stance, Twirl BME To Left Hand, BME Held Horizontally In Front
Charyut BME to Right Side as Right Foot Steps To Closed Stance

Note: These can be done as partner drills - Attack 1 vs Defense 1.
Left handed students can do all on left side.

ProTech Weapons Ssahng Jeol Bong

The Ssahng Jeol Bong (also know as the *Nunchaku, chucks* or *chain sticks*) area weapon which traditionally consists of 2 wooden short sticks connected by a chain. In the ProTech fighting system, we practice with a safety weapon and do not recommend using the wooden version at the colored belt level.

The popular belief is that the Ssahng Jeol Bong was originally a short Southeast Asian flail used to thresh rice or soybeans (that is, separate the grain from the husk). It is possible that it was developed in response to the moratorium on edged weaponry under kings law in the 17th century, and that the weapon was most likely conceived and used exclusively for that end as peasant farmers were forbidden conventional weaponry such as arrows or blades so they improvised using only what they had available, farm tools such as the sickle.

Master Club Curriculum - SJB Basics

Single Ssahng Jeol Bong Basics

Basic	Description
1	Triangle
2	High/Low Ready Position
3	Figure 8
4	Nine Angles of Strikes
5	V Strike
6	Reverse Figure 8
7	X-Strike
8	360° Horizontal Twirl
9	Lasso
10	Propeller Strike
11	Front Neck Circle
12	Vertical Handover (Over Shoulder)
13	Underarm X-Strike
14	360° Vertical Around Leg (Over the String)
15	Kick Up (Behind back and kick up with opposite leg)

Notes: Only required to do favorite hand - Left handed students can perform mirror image. Tigers: Only 1-5, K4K: Only 1-12, Adults: All

Master Club Curriculum - SJB Form

Colored Belt Ssahng Jeol Bong Form

Form Pattern

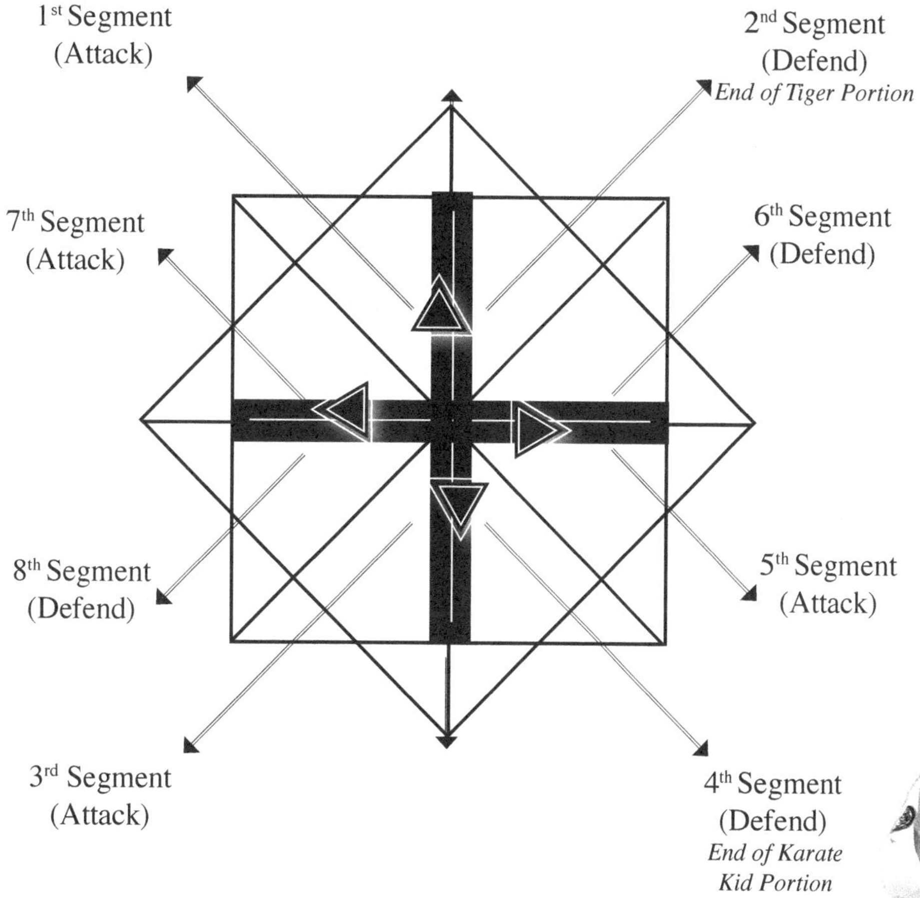

- 1st Segment (Attack)
- 2nd Segment (Defend) — *End of Tiger Portion*
- 7th Segment (Attack)
- 6th Segment (Defend)
- 8th Segment (Defend)
- 5th Segment (Attack)
- 3rd Segment (Attack)
- 4th Segment (Defend) — *End of Karate Kid Portion*

Rev 4.0 - © KarateBuilt L.L.C.

Master Club Curriculum - SJB Form

Colored Belt Ssahng Jeol Bong Form

Charyut Closed Stance, SJB At Right Side Held Down To Side.
Ready Step Right Foot To Parallel Stance, Catch SJB In Left Hand (Hands By Belt Knot)

Move	Technique
1	Right Foot Steps Forward (East) To Fighting Stance, High / Low Ready Position
2	Triangle
3	Figure 8 (Finish With SJB On Right Shoulder
4	Turn To West (Simple Turn, Feet Just Shift), Line 1 Strike
5	Triangle
6	Reverse Figure 8 – Kihap (End Of Tiny Tiger Portion)
7	Step Right Foot To West, V-Strike
8	Triangle
9	X-Strike
10	Turn To East (Simple Turn, Feet Just Shift), Line 1 Strike
11	360° Horizontal Twirl (Smoothly Into…)
12	Lasso (Behind The Back – End With Twirl Up To Left Shoulder) – Kihap (End Of Karate Kid Portion)
13	Step Right Foot To Right (South), Front Neck Circle
14	Triangle
15	Vertical Handover
16	Turn To North (Simple Turn, Feet Just Shift), Underarm X-Strike (To Left Shoulder)
17	Left Triangle
18	Underarm X-Strike (To Right Shoulder)
19	Step Right Foot Forward To North, V-Strike
20	Triangle
21	360° Vertical Around Leg
22	Turn To South, Line 1 Strike (Strike To Waist On Turn, And Right Into…)
23	Kick Up (Catch With Right)
24	Twirl Up To Right – Kihap

Bahroh Step Right Foot To Parallel Stance, Catch SJB in Left Hand (Hands By Belt Knot)
Charyut SJB Snap to one hand, and to Right Side as Right Foot Steps To Closed Stance

Note: These can not be done as partner drills. Left handed students can do all on left side.

REV 4.0 - © KarateBuilt L.L.C.

Master Club

Colored Belt SPARRING

Sparring

Sparring is an important and very fun part of your training. This is when you will start to learn applications of techniques you have previously learned, and develop the skills to respond automatically to an attack. A set of THREE reaction drills will be assigned for each graduation to practice defense, counter attack and offensive skills. You will need to bring the following to *every* class (whether you think we will be sparring or not); ATA Approved Safety Gear (Feet, Hand, Headgear, Chest Protector), Mouthpiece, Cup (for Men). To keep your sparring experience safe and fun, we always use proper safety gear and all sparring is supervised by instructors. Have FUN!!

Sparring Reaction Drills
(subject to improvement)

Drill A
Defense Drill: Side Kick when attacker advances
Counter Drill: When Opponent Butterfly Kick, Reverse Side Kick
Offense Drill: Butterfly Kick (step forward jump spin Round Kick)

Drill B
Defense Drill: Back leg slide (1/2 stance) on attack Round Kick
Counter Drill: Back leg slide, #2 Round Kick
Offense Drill: #3 Jump Axe Kick, follow with Punch (set up - #2 Front Kick)

Drill C
Defense Drill: Footwork Practice (Move direction foot 1st)
Counter Drill: Retreating Jump Reverse Side Kick
Offense Drill: Close Distance with Punching (Jam)

Drill D
Defense Drill: Fade Back #2 Jump Round Kick on attacker advance
Counter Drill: Block Attacker Round Kick, Punch, Reverse Side Kick
Offense Drill: Double Switch, #1 Jump Forward RK

Drill E
Defense Drill: X-Step when attacker advances
Counter Drill: X-Step, Reverse Side Kick (or 45° Reverse Side Kick)
Offense Drill: Multiple #1 Round Kick Low Then #1 Round Kick High

Drill F
Defense Drill: Dodge to Open Side when attacker advances
Counter Drill: When Opponent #1 Round Kick, Reverse Side Kick (repeat for Opponent #1 Front Kick)
Offense Drill: Cross Gap, Front Back Fist, Reverse Punch, #2 Round Kick

Rev 4.0 - © KarateBuilt L.L.C.

My Notes on My Road to Master

Master Club
Colored Belt
BREAKING

Board Breaking

Board breaking is designed to be a safe way to practice application of power in techniques. It's better to break a board than practice on each other! Other benefits of board breaking training include focus (you must focus on the target to break it), proper execution (only through proper technique will you break the board), power (you must kihap!) and most importantly, attitude (board breaking is largely a mental exercise). Our instructors will guide you through to Black Belt Excellence!

Master Club Curriculum - Breaks

Colored Belt Board Breaks

A Breaks (when training on IW1)
  Reverse Side Kick
  Horizontal Elbow Strike

B Breaks (when training on CJ2)
  Round Kick
  Palm Heel Strike

C Breaks (when training on SA5)
  Front Kick
  Ridgehand Strike

D Breaks (when training on CJ1)
  Step Together Jump Side Kick
  Upset Knifehand Strike

E Breaks (when training on IW2)
  Hook Kick
  Upward Elbow Strike

F Breaks (when training on SA4)
  Side Kick
  Knifehand Strike

Board Color Guidelines

The color of board required is listed below. This is only a guide, however and students may be asked to break lighter or heavier boards based on instructor recommendation.

Age	Color	Age	Color
Under 7	White	11-12	Green
7-8	Yellow	13-15	Blue
9-10	Orange	16+ Female	Blue
		16+ Male	Brown

*Obstacle requirements are based on student size, age and rank.

Master Club

Black Belt Curriculum

Master Club
Black Belt Uniform Requirements

Black Belt Uniform Requirements

As a Black Belt you are required to look your best in the Academy. If you are part of the Leadership Program your uniform will have:

- A Leadership Collar (Red to Black for Adults, Red/White/Blue for Kids).
- Name on the back of uniform.
- Optional XTreme ATA Uniform.

If you are not in Leadership Training yet your uniform will have:

- A Student Black Bottom Stripe.
- No name on the back of the uniform.

T-shirts may be worn on designated days only.

Master Club

Black Belt Fitness Requirements

Master Club Curriculum - Fitness

Name: _____

Graduation Date: __/__/__

Black Belt Fitness Requirements

The ATA-Fit standards are below. To advance in rank, Black Belts must be in the top 20% of fitness for their age range **or** show improvement (in total number) between this test and the next rank test.

Pushups (Males)

<10	10-13	14-17	18-29	30-39	40-49	50-59	60+	Percentile
25	30	45	62	52	40	39	38	99%
20	25	40	47	39	30	25	23	80%
15	20	35	37	30	24	19	18	60%
10	15	30	29	24	18	13	10	40%

Pushups (Females)

Percentile	<10	10-13	14-17	18-29	30-39	40-49	50-59	60+
99%	20	25	30	42	39	20	15	12
80%	15	20	25	28	23	15	13	9
60%	10	15	20	21	15	13	9	6
40%	5	10	15	15	11	9	6	3

Situps (Males)

<10	10-13	14-17	18-29	30-39	40-49	50-59	60+	Percentile
40	45	50	55	51	47	43	39	99%
35	40	45	47	43	39	35	30	80%
30	35	40	42	39	34	28	22	60%
25	30	35	38	35	29	24	19	40%

Situps (Females)

Percentile	<10	10-13	14-17	18-29	30-39	40-49	50-59	60+
99%	35	40	45	51	42	38	30	28
80%	25	35	40	44	35	29	24	17
60%	20	30	35	38	29	24	20	11
40%	15	25	30	32	25	20	14	6

1999. The Cooper Institute for Aerobics Research

Additionally the fitness test includes:
- Kicks (feet) Techniques
- Hand Techniques
- Combination Techniques

Each of the five areas are to be done for one minute with a one minute rest between each (10 minutes total). The total score (Pushups + Situps + Kicks + Hands + Combinations) determines your passing ability. The passing number will be determined at graduation. The next page is a sample fitness test form.

Rev 4.0 - © KarateBuilt L.L.C.

FITNESS TEST

To advance in rank, all of our Black Belts must be in the top 20% of fitness for their age range or show improvement (in total number) between this test and the next rank test.

Name		
Academy		
Rank Testing For		
Pushups		
Situps		
Foot Techniques		
Combinations		
Hand Techniques		
TOTAL		

ATA FIT

Master Club

Black Belt Open Hand Curriculum

Rev 4.0 - © KarateBuilt L.L.C.

My Notes on My Road to Master

Master Club Curriculum - PPCT

Name: _____

Graduation Date: __/__/__

Pressure Point Control Tactics (PPCT)

Master Club Curriculum - PPCT

ProTech Vital Pressure Points

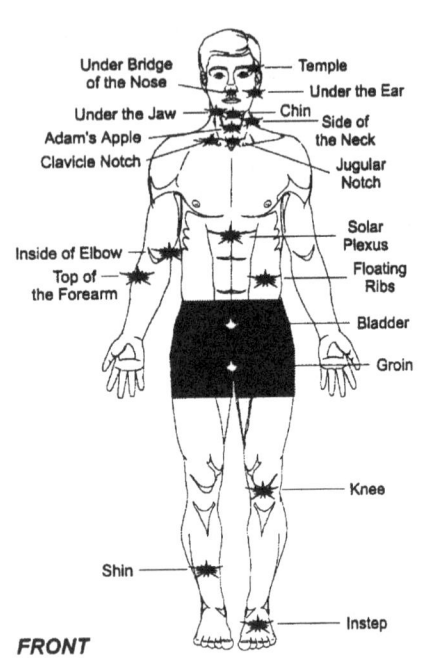
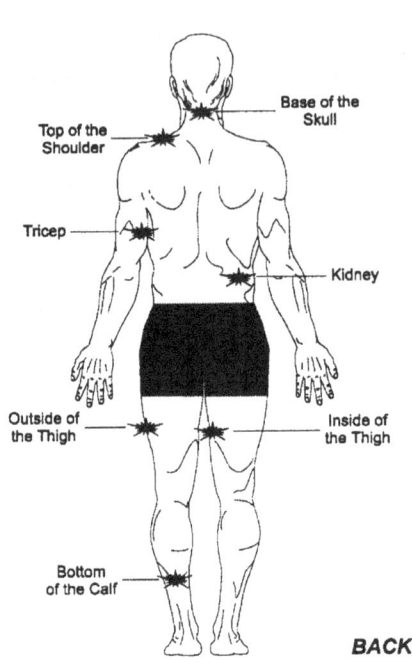

ProTech Striking Pressure Points

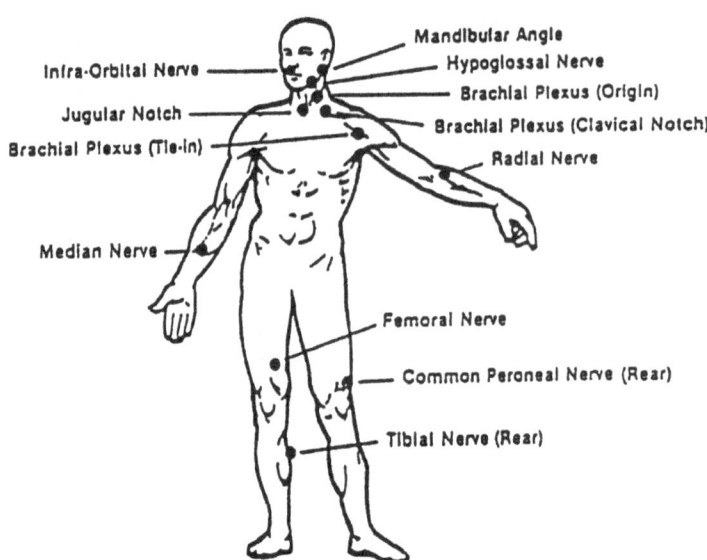

PPCT Flow (Inside)

Attacker: Punch
Defender: Step to inside, Then
Outer Forearm Block with Brachial Plexus Tie In Stun
    (Note: Blocking hand will grab attacker's punching arm)
Upward Elbow Strike to Bicep
Brachial Plexus Origin Stun
Attacker: Punch with other arm
Defender: Block (still holding original punching arm)
Brachial Plexus Origin Stun to Other Side of Neck
Grab head with free hand (still holding original punching arm)
Knee Strike
Take Down (by pushing head down)
Optional: Wrist Lock to stable position

PPCT Flow (Outside)

Attacker: Punch
Defender: Step to outside, Then
Double Pass
Double Hammerfist Strike
Supported Elbow to Radial Nerve on Bicep
Brachial Plexus Origin Stun
Arm Wrench
Knee to Common Peroneal
Arm Bar
Leg Over Head, Break Arm

Rev 4.0 - © KarateBuilt L.L.C.

My Notes on My Road to Master

Master Club Curriculum - JL

Name: _____
Graduation Date: __/__/__

Joint Locks

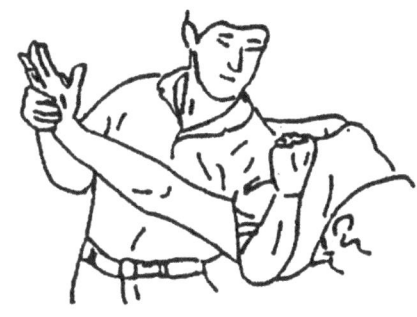

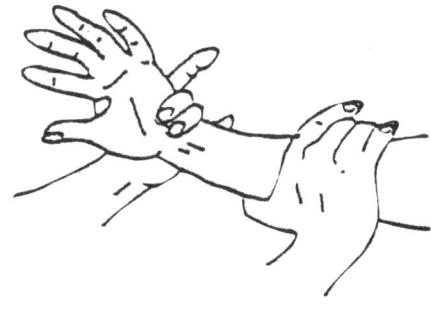
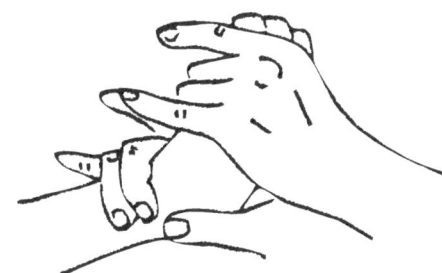
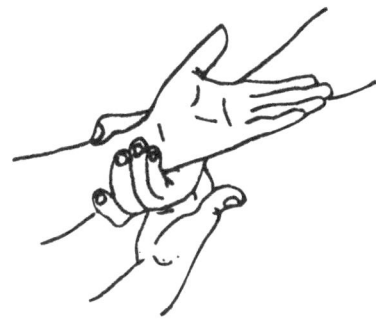
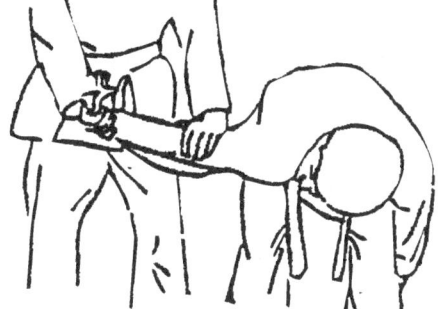

Joint Lock Basics (A)

Circular Wrist Lock
Circle hand around opponents wrist and grab wrist. (Cross hand grip)

Double Hand Wrist Lock
Used to lock opponent's wrist or break away. (Cross hand grip)

Bicep Arm Lock
When punched, check block with same side hand, opposite hand bends elbow in to arm lock. **Escape**: Push up on opponent elbow.

Straight Arm Bar
Pressure is applied just below the elbow to control the opponent. Entry to arm bar can be from any grab.

Counter Arm Bar
When in the arm bar position, grab opponent hand, pull through and counter with Arm Bar.

Gooseneck
Apply this technique from a Straight Arm Bar. For a more secure lock, pin the opponent's thumb to their arm. **Escape #1**: Palm down. **Escape #2**: Push palm up, turn trapped hand to grab opponent, pull down to arm bar.

Chicken Wing
Be sure to maintain constant pressure on the opponent's wrist while applying this technique. Keep your opponent's arm tight to your body for a more effective lock. **Escape**: Grab opponent's wrist, pull opponent's arm off trapped hand.

Joint Locks – Flow (A)

Attacker (A): Punch

Defender (D): Bicep Arm Lock

A): Push Up, Armbar

D): Counter Armbar

A): Counter Armbar, Gooseneck

D): Counter Armbar, Gooseneck

A): Counter Armbar

D): Counter Armbar

A): Counter Armbar, Gooseneck

D): Escape – Push Down, Retreat at Arm Base

See diagram on following page.

Joint Lock Flow Drill #1 (A)

(A) punch (B) bicep arm lock

(A) elbow push

(A) straight arm bar

(B) counter straight arm bar

(A) counter with straight arm bar, follow with a gooseneck

(B) counter gooseneck

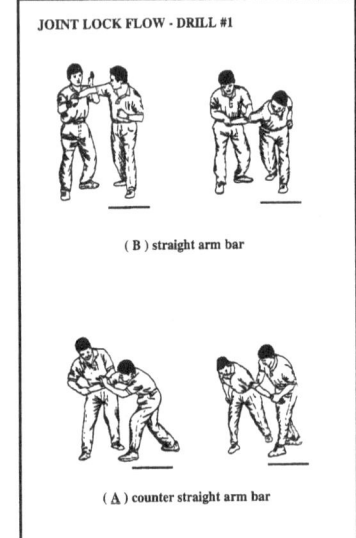

(B) straight arm bar

(A) counter straight arm bar

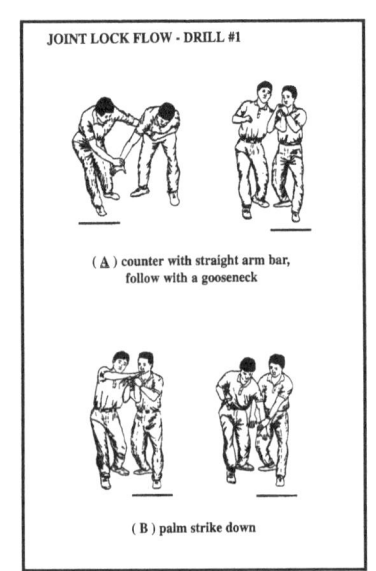

(A) counter with straight arm bar, follow with a gooseneck

(B) palm strike down

Master Club Curriculum - Joint Locks

Joint Lock Basics (B)

Lunch Money
Open hand and lift, other hand peels opponent off. (parallel grip) (Serious Lunch Money - reinforce with other hand)

Shooting Gun
Hand (webbing/shooting gun) circles around opponent arm. (parallel grip)

Indian Burn
Each hand moves in opposite circular directions.

Bow
Near hand presses opponent's hand to chest, Other hand pushes down with body.

Nine Block
When punched, nine block.

Straight Arm Bar
Pressure is applied just below the elbow to control the opponent. This can lead to the Hammerlock.

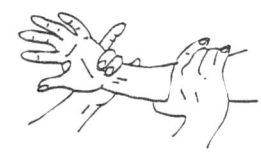

Hammerlock
For the basic application of the hammerlock, start with your opponent in a straight arm bar, As you apply the hammerlock, be sure to keep your opponent close to your body and pull back on his chin or shoulder to keep a solid hold on him. **Escape** #1: Grab opponents elbow and pull up to lock elbow. This escape can be countered by a palm heel to their shoulder. **Escape** #2: "Snake" free arm behind body into where opponent is locking arm.

Counter Arm Bar
When in the arm bar position, grab opponent hand, pull through and counter with Arm Bar.

Eagle Wing
Similar to the Arm Bar, except Pressure goes all the way up to the opponent's shoulder.

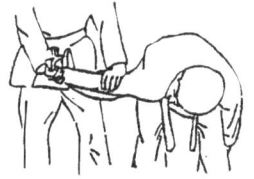

Rev 4.0 - © KarateBuilt L.L.C.

Joint Locks – Flow (B)

Attacker (A): Punch

Defender (D): 9 Block into Hammerlock

A): Escape Counter Hammerlock (Push up on D's elbow or own arm)

D): Palm Strike to Brachial Plexus Tie In

A): Trap Palm, Straight Armbar, to Hammerlock

D): Escape Counter Hammerlock (Push up on D's elbow or own arm)

A): Palm Strike to Brachial Plexus Tie In

D): Trap Palm, Straight Armbar, Side Kick to A's Knee, Retreat at Arm Base

See diagram on following page.

Master Club Curriculum - Joint Locks

Joint Lock Flow Drill #2 (B)

FRONT VIEW **REAR VIEW**   **FRONT VIEW** **REAR VIEW**

 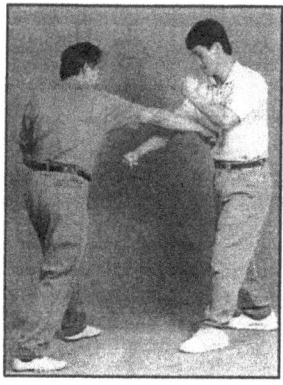  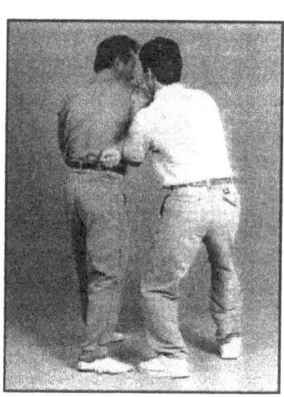

1 Punch

4 Hammer Lock

2 Nine Block into Hammer Lock

5 Escape Counter Attack

 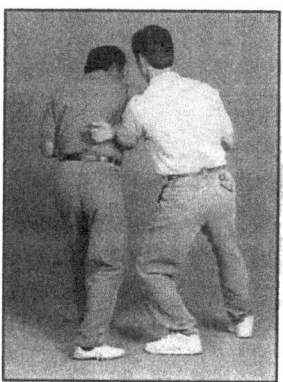 

3 Hammer Lock

6 Escape Counter attack

Master Club Curriculum - Joint Locks

Joint Lock Flow Drill #2 (B) (part 2)

FRONT VIEW   **REAR VIEW**   **FRONT VIEW**   **REAR VIEW**

7 *Palm Strike (Brachial Plexus Tie-in)*

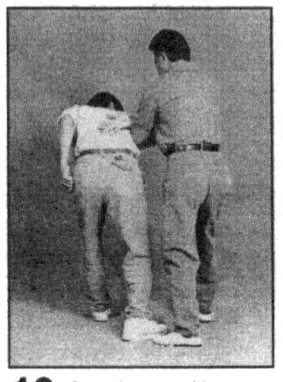

10 *Arm bar to Hammer Lock*

8 *Straight Arm Bar*

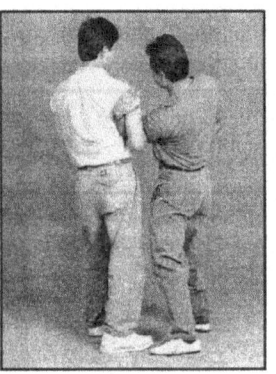

11 *Counter Attack*

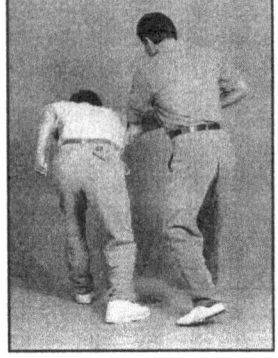

9 *Straight Arm Bar*

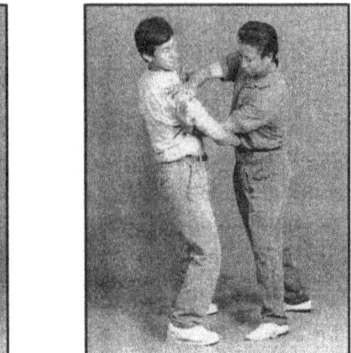

12 *Palm Strike (Brachial Plexus Tie-in)*

Rev 4.0 - © KarateBuilt L.L.C.

Master Club Curriculum - Joint Locks

Joint Lock Flow Drill #2 (B) (part 3)

FRONT VIEW **REAR VIEW** **FRONT VIEW** **REAR VIEW**

 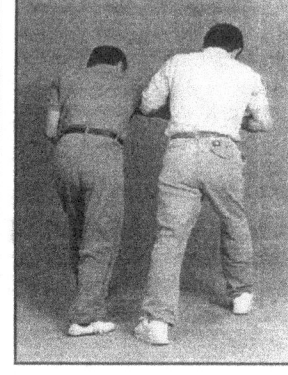  

13 Straight Arm Bar   **14** Side Kick

Master Club Curriculum - Joint Locks

Additional Material
Joint Lock Basics - Parallel Grip

Lunch Money
Used to break the opponent's wrist.

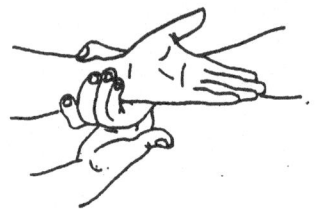

Shooting Gun
Used to break the opponent's wrist.

Bow
The Bow technique begins from the Indian Burn. It is very important to keep a stable and straight posture. Bend the opponent's elbow for a more controlled application.

Straight Arm Bar
Pressure is applied just above the elbow to control the opponent.

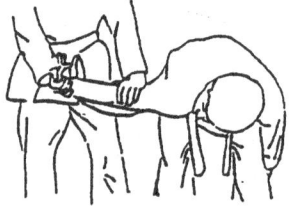

Indian Burn
Hand and wrist are turned against each other.

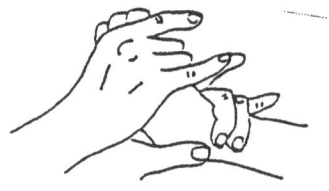

Eagle Wing
This technique is a variation of the Straight Arm Bar. Instead of putting pressure on your opponent's elbow with your hand or forearm, you come down with the full weight of your body against his elbow/shoulder.

Additional Material
Joint Lock Basics - Cross Hand Grip

Circular Wrist Lock
Circle hand outside under opponents hand and back to inside to break grip

Double Hand Wrist Lock
Used to lock opponent's wrist or break away

Straight Arm Bar
Pressure is applied just below the elbow to control the opponent.

Hammerlock
For the basic application of the hammerlock, start with your opponent in a straight arm bar, As you apply the hammerlock, be sure to keep your opponent close to your body and pull back on his chin or shoulder to keep a solid hold on him

Gooseneck
Apply this technique from a Straight Arm Bar. For a more secure lock, pin the opponent's thumb to their arm.

Chicken Wing
Be sure to maintain constant pressure on the opponent's wrist while applying this technique. Keep your opponent's arm tight to your body for a more effective lock.

Master Club Curriculum - Joint Locks

Additional Material
Joint Lock Flow Drill (C)

Attacker
Shake Hands and Punch

Defender
Use Attackers Arm to Block and...
Duck Underneath Attackers Arm
Hammerlock with Shoulder Lockup

Attacker
Escape to Arm Bar
Gooseneck

Defender
Escape Gooseneck (Grab Attacker's Hand and Pull Away)
Backfist (still Holding Hand)
Arm Bar Takedown

Spontaneous Knife Defense System

Six Knife Defense Lines of Attack

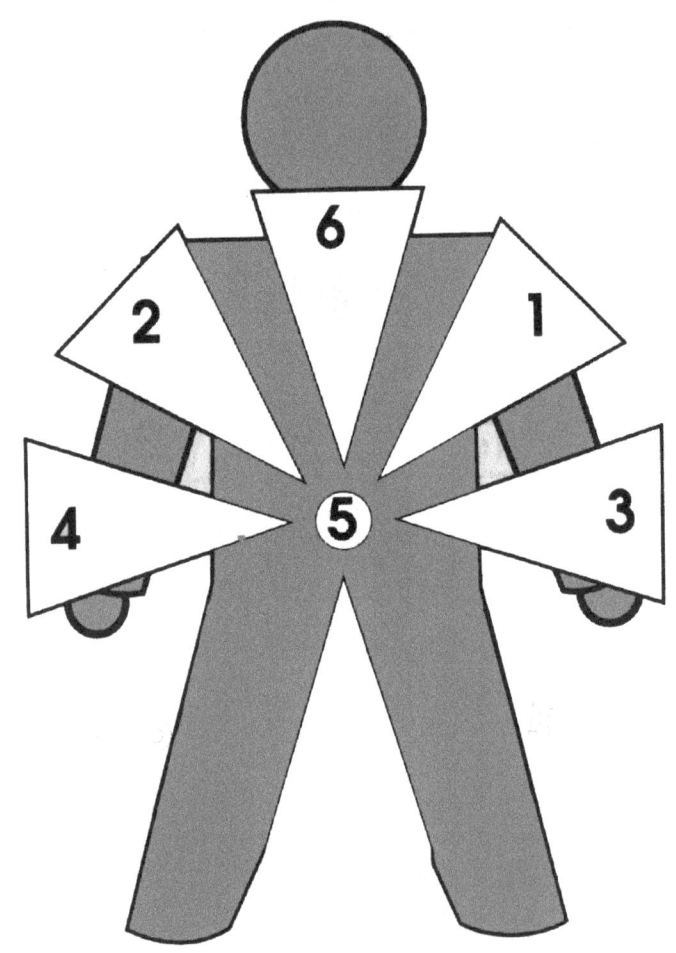

Knife Defense has six lines of attack. There are two line 5's: line 5 low to the stomach, line 5 high to chest).

Master Club Curriculum - Knife Defense

Spontaneous Knife Defense System

Initial Defense for Attack

Attack Line #1
Check (arm up); Pass

Attack Line #2
Double Stop

Attack Line #3
Check (arm down); Pass

Attack Line #4
Low / High Stop (similar to low X-Block to side)

Attack Line #5 (low)
Double pass (fingers down)

Attack Line #5 (high)
Double pass (fingers up)

Attack Line #6
Double pass (fingers up)

Follow Up

All Attack Lines (after Initial Defense)
Grab behind elbow (knife hand), elbow strike to lower part of bicep (radial nerve); brachial stun; wrist throw takedown; elbow strike to break wrist; retrieve knife.

My Notes on My Road to Master

MC Curriculum - Ground Fighting

Name: _____
Graduation Date: ___/___/___

Ground Fighting

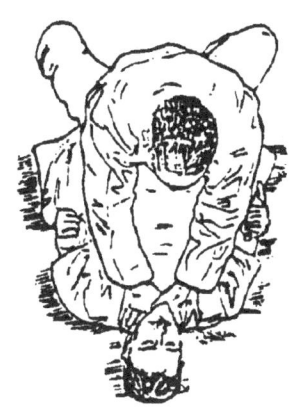

Master Club Curriculum - Ground Fighting

Ground Fighting Basics (A)

Mount Position
In the mount position, the attacker is straddling the defender.

Guard Position
In the guard position defender is on their back and the attacker is between the defender's legs.

Standing Takedown – Front Leg Sweep
On attacker's punch, block and step past attacker (inside leg passes attacker). Front leg sweeps attackers leg, while hands guide attacker to ground. Optional: defender proceeds to Mount Position.

Hip Thrust
With attacker on top in Mounted position, defender pushes hips up to move attacker forward over defender. This is usually followed up by a "Swim Out" reversal.

"Swim Out" Reversal
With Attacker on top in Mounted position, defender extends hands up and around the outside of the attackers arms "swimming" to lock attacker down to defender's body. defender traps the outside of the attacker's foot and rolls over to be on top of attacker. **Safety:** Make sure attacker closes hands into a fist before rolling.

Side Arm Bar
Defender is on bottom, traps hand and slides same side leg over attacker's head. Roll attacker to outside (keeping hand) and (making sure body is in tight to attacker) thrust hips up and pull back on attacker's hand (keep attacker's thumb pointed up).

On Ground Kick
In Crab Position, Balance with opposite leg & hand, kick with other leg and hand up. **Return to Standing**: Kicking leg, slides behind, and stand up (hand stays in front at all times).

Ground Fighting Drill (A)

Attacker (A):
Step forward, right lunge punch.

Defender (D):
Block, step forward right foot behind attacker. Standing takedown (front leg sweep). Continue to mount position, Start punching.

Attacker (A):
Blocking (cover head), Grab lapel and hip thrust. "Swim Out" reversal to guard position. Start choking Defender.

Defender (D):
Wedge knees, then feet to resist choke. Grab 1 arm, kick leg over to side arm bar.

Repeat with roles reversed.

Ground Fighting Basics (B)

Mount Position
In the mount position, the attacker is straddling the defender.

Mount Position (Facing Down)
The attacker is on top of the defender's back. Attacker may put defender into choke hold.

Guard Position
In the guard position defender is on their back and the attacker is between the defender's legs.

Trip
When attacker is standing up and reaching, defender (on side) puts lower foot behind attacker's ankle and upper foot kicks out at knee of attacker.

Shoot Defense
Both standing: when attacker "shoots" for feet, defender hops back and presses with forearm on attacker back (so attacker will not be able to reach defender feet). This can be followed up by defender pressing all the way to the ground and into mount position (facing down).

Triangle
When attacker is in guard, defender traps 1 arm, and pulls to get legs up to attacker's neck and forms a "triangle" with one leg bent around attacker's neck and the other bent around their own foot.

"Swim Out" Reversal
With Attacker on top in Mounted position, defender extends hands up and around the outside of the attackers arms "swimming" to lock attacker down to defender's body. defender traps the outside of the attacker's foot and rolls over to be on top of attacker. **Safety:** Make sure attacker closes hands into a fist before rolling.

Ground Fighting Drill (B)

Attacker (A):
Shoots for defender's legs.

Defender (D):
Shoot defense, press to ground, mount from behind (mount position, both facing down). Attempt to apply choke.

Attacker (A):
Cover head, swim under & press out and escape, mount on top.

Defender (D):
"Swim out" reverse to guard and press A's legs down to mount.

Attacker (A):
"Swim out" reverse to guard.

Defender (D):
Squeeze Legs together and push A out.

Attacker (A):
Attempt to press D's legs down to mount.

Defender (D):
As A is attempting, trap arm, swing opposite leg (of arm) over A's arm and around neck, other leg is bent around ankle forming triangle.

Repeat with roles reversed.

Master Club Curriculum - Ground Fighting

Additional Material
Ground Fighting - Drill #1

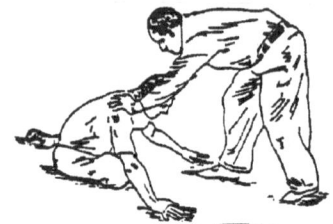

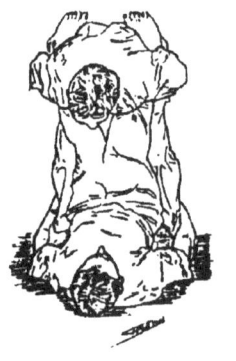

Additional Material
Ground Fighting - Drill #2

1. **Head lock from the side:** With your outside hand, push away the attacker's bottom arm; lean back with your arms spread wide while placing your knee behind the attacker's legs to displace his balance.

2. **Head lock from the side with punch:** Use your free hand to push away punch; grab attacker's arm that is around your neck with your free hand and pull his other arm to his back with your other hand while pushing behind attacker's knee with your knee and leaning back to displace his balance.

3. **Head lock from the rear:** Pull down on attacker's forearm while spinning clockwise to displace his balance and break the hold.

4. **Head lock from rear:** Pull down on attacker's forearm while bending forward, pulling the attacker off the ground.

5. **Head lock from the side:** Turn clockwise to face the attacker and push on his far side with your right hand and pull him toward you with your other hand to displace his balance and release the hold

6. **Head lock from the side:** With your inside leg, push attacker's outside leg forward while stepping back to the rear, causing him to fall to the ground.

7. **Head lock from the ground with the attacker on top:** Bring your top leg over the attacker's side and reach with your top arm over his outside shoulder; bring yourself over and on top of your attacker.

8. **Head lock from the ground with the attacker on top:** Bring your top arm in front of the attacker's face, push his head back and finish with your top leg over his head.

9. **Head lock from the ground with the attacker on top:** Bring your top arm over the top of the attacker's outside shoulder and place your hand on the ground while shifting your weight to the front, the top of your head will be on the ground with your attacker under you.

Additional Material
Ground Fighting - Drill #3

1. **With attacker on top of you, hitting you in the face:** Use a hip thrust to throw him forward and off of you.

2. **With attacker on top of you, preparing to throw a punch toward your face:** Reach up and push him on the same side he's punching with to push him off the opposite side he was punching with.

3. **With attacker on top, choking you:** Use a hip thrust to throw him off you.

4. **After throwing attacker forward with a hip thrust:** Slide up to free your arms, then reach around the outside of him arms to trap them and roll to the side placing your attacker on the bottom.

5. **Attacker on top choking you:** Turn to side and push off your attacker with your right leg to slide forward on your left side, bring your left leg to the outside of his knee and your right leg to his other side to throw him over.

6. **Attacker on top choking:** Bring your leg up and over attacker's shoulders and place it under your other leg; use your other leg to secure the hold while pulling his trapped hand into an arm bar.

7. **Attacker across your body, punching you in the side:** You try to roll over, attacker pushes your knee down and gets back in the mounted position on top of you.

8. **Standing clench, face to face, with attacker's arm around your neck:** Wrap your right arm around the back of his neck, and use your left arm to reinforce the hold by placing your right hand in the bend of your left arm and placing your left hand behind your neck.

9. **Facing each other, attacker grabs you around your waist:** With your left arm in front of his chin and your right arm behind his neck, bring your right arm inside your left arm, and push back with your left hand to displace his balance.

10. **Head grab from the front:** While bracing down against the top of the attacker's shoulder with your higher arm, push against his leg with your lower arm to "stretch" him.

REV 4.0 - © KarateBuilt L.L.C.

Master Club Curriculum - Ground Fighting

Additional Material
Ground Fighting - Drill #3

My Notes on My Road to Master

Combatives

Master Club Curriculum - Combatives

Combative Training

Notes:
Combatives are designed to build strength and fighting skills. They are to be done with bag gloves and a partner holding "mitts" such as the ATA curved mitts. The partner will initiate the combative - that is, they will "Feed" the person doing the combative - typically with alternating right and left attacks on the odd and even sides respectfully.

Stage 1: Individual - Combative Open to Front
Stage 2: Alternate Paired (7, then 8...)
Stage 3: Partner Calling Out Combative Number Prior to "Feed"
Stage 4: Adding Base Drills to Pairs
Stage 5: Random

Base Drills:
Combatives 1-6 are the "Base" Drills. These are done every cycle

Paired Drills:
Combatives 7 and up are "Paired Drills". These are rotated and to be done in conjunction with the "Base" Drills.

Master Club Curriculum - Combatives

Drill	Attacker	Defender (Combative)
1	Feed Right	Jab
2	Feed Left	Jab, Cross
3	Feed Right	Cross, Hook, Cross
4	Feed Left	Jab, Cross, Hook, Cross
5	Feed Right for Uppercut	Right Uppercut, Hook, Cross, Uppercut
6	Feed Left for Uppercut	Left Uppercut, Cross, Hook, Uppercut
7	Right Attack (to D Left)	Slip to Left, Hook, Cross, Hook
8	Left Attack (to D Right)	Slip to Right, Cross, Hook, Cross
9	Right Punch	Pass/Deflect (body shifts to Left), Right Cross (5th Rib), Left Hook
10	Left Punch	Pass/Deflect (body shifts to right), Straight Jab (5th Rib) Overhand Right
11	Right Hook Low, Right Hook High	Cover 1st Hook, Slip, Liver, Hook, Cross
12	Left Hook Low, Left Hook High	Cover 1st Hook, Slip, Kidney, Uppercut, Jab, Cross
13	RK from Left (A's Right Leg)	Leg Block, Cross, Hook, Right RK (Low)
14	RK from Right (A's Left Leg)	Leg Block, Hook, Cross, Switch, Left RK (Low)
15	Right Attack (to D Left)	Right ES, Spin Left ES, Right ES, Grab, Knee (position 1)
16	Left Attack (to D Right)	Left Hook, Spin Right ES, Left ES, Grab, Knee (position 3)
17	Right Attack (to D Left)	#1 Leg (Left) FK, #2 RK (Right) – Replace position, Rev SK (Right)
18	Left Attack (to D Right)	#2 Leg (Right) FK – Replace position, Switch #2 RK (Left) – Replace position, Rev SK (Left) – Can advance instead of switching

Rev 4.0 - © KarateBuilt L.L.C.

My Notes on My Road to Master

Master Club

1° Black Belt Curriculum

1° Black Belt to 2° Black Belt Rank Requirements:

Forms are the foundation of Songahm Taekwondo. Each consists of techniques and movements that are designed to improve a student's coordination, balance, stamina and strength. This guide is for reference. Your instructor will instruct you in how to perform the forms. If you try and learn forms just from this guide, you risk learning them incorrectly and forming a bad habit. Remember the old saying "Practice Makes Perfect" is wrong! Practice makes <u>habits</u> (maybe good ones, maybe bad ones). Only *<u>Perfect Practice Makes Perfect</u>*! Good luck on your road to Mastery!!

My Road to Mastery!

2° Black Belt Planner:

Take a minute and plan your road to 2° Black Belt. Your instructor can help you find the correct testing dates. You should plan on testing every 2 months.

Current Rank	Testing For:	Requirements:*	Graduation Fee:**	My Test Date
1° R	1°D	Instructor Permission, 2 Months of Classes, Current Form, Black Belt Level Free Sparring Board Breaks and *Leadership* Attitude! Level 1 and 2 ProTech Basics, Board Breaks at Graduation	$80	__/__/__
1° D	Midterm #1	Instructor Permission, 2 Months at Rank, Current 1/2 Shim Jun, Sparring, Currrent ProTech Requirements	$80	__/__/__
1° D	Midterm #2	Instructor Permission, 4 Months at Rank, Current 1/2 Shim Jun, Sparring, Currrent ProTech Requirements	$80	__/__/__
1° D	Midterm #3	Instructor Permission, 6 Months at Rank, Shim Jun, Sparring, Board Breaks, Currrent ProTech Requirements	$80	__/__/__
1° D	Midterm #4	Instructor Permission, 8 Months at Rank, Shim Jun, Sparring, Board Breaks, Currrent ProTech Requirements	$80	__/__/__
1° D	Midterm #5	Instructor Permission, 10 Months at Rank, Shim Jun, Sparring, Board Breaks, Currrent ProTech Requirements	$80	__/__/__
1° D	2°R	Instructor Permission, 1 Year at Rank, Shim Jun, Sparring, Board Breaks **at Graduation**, Currrent ProTech Requirements	$80	__/__/__
2° R	Midterm	Instructor Permission, 2 Months at Rank, Shim Jun, New Board Breaks, Current 2°R ProTech Requirements	$80	__/__/__
2° R	2°D	Instructor Permission, 4 Months at Rank, Shim Jun, New Board Breaks **at Graduation**, Sparring, Current 2°R ProTech Requirements	$80	__/__/__

*2 Ssahng Jeol Bongs and 2 Bahng Mahng Ees, Jahng Bong and Chest Protector Required for Master Club Classes. All Requirements subject to change. *Graduation for rank can only be done at a designated Black Belt Boot Camp - no exceptions!*

**Graduation fees and requirements subject to change.

Rev 4.0 - © KarateBuilt L.L.C.

Master Club 1° Black Belt
ProTech Material Rotation

January	March	May	July	September	November
BME Use of Weapon & Combat Drills	BME Form	SJB Use of Weapon & Combat Drills	SJB Form	Knife Defense & Use of Knife	Knife Form
Graduation	Graduation	Graduation	Graduation	Graduation	Graduation

Required Equipment*

Korean Name	Common Name	Abbreviation	Required
Ssahng Jeol Bong	Nunchaku	SJB	Two Required
Bahng Mahng Ee	Stick	BME	Two Required
Practice Knife	Knife	Knife	One Required

* For your safety, all equipment must be American Taekwondo Association / ProTech approved

Name: _____

Graduation Date: __/__/__

Shim Jun
"Begin Planting Seeds for the Future"

Your form is on the following pages. These are reprinted by permission of the American Taekwondo Association

The pattern of the form is as follows:

Master Club Curriculum - Forms

Shim Jun

Step	Side	Technique	Stance	Section
1	Left	Double Inner Forearm Block	Middle	High
2	Right	Upset Punch	Middle	High
3	Left	Upset Palmheel Block	Middle	High
4	Right	Punch	Middle	Middle
5	Left	Punch	Middle	Middle
6	Left	Advanced Double Knifehand Block	Back	High
7	Left	Circular Dbl Knifehand Low Block	Back	Low
8	Right	Stomp Kick	Middle	Low
9	Right	Back Fist	Middle	High
10	Right	#3 Side Kick		Mid/High
11	Right	High/Low Block	Closed	High/Low
12	Left	High/Low Block	Closed	Hgh/Low
13	Right	Knifehand Low Block	Rear	Low
14	Right	#1 Front Kick		Mid/High
15	Right	Step Togther #1 Jump Hook Kick		Mid/High
16	Right	Nine Block	Sparing	Mid/Low
17	Right	Double Inner Form Block	Middle	Middle
18	Left	Upset Punch	Middle	Middle
19	Right	Upset Palmheel Block	Middle	High
20	Left	Punch	Middle	Middle
21	Right	Punch - Ki-hap	Middle	Middle
22	Right	Adv Double Knifehand Block	Back	High
23	Right	Circular Dbl Knifehand Block	Back	Low
24	Left	Stomp Kick	Middle	Low
25	Left	Back Fist	Middle	High
26	Left	#3 Side Kick		Mid/High
27	L/R	X-Block	Closed	Low
28	L/R	Head Grab	Closed	High
29	Right	Knee Strike		Middle
30	Left	Knifehand Low Block	Rear	Low

Shim Jun (2nd Part)

Step	Side	Technique	Stance	Section
31	Left	#1 Front Kick		Mid/High
32	Left	Step Together #1 Jump Hook Kick		Mid/High
33	Left	Nine Block	Sparring	Mid/Low
34	Right	Square Block (L - fist, R - knifehand)	Back	High
35	Right	Upset Knifehand Strike	Back	High
36	Left	Reverse Vertical Punch	Front	Middle
37	Right	#3 Jump Front Kick		Mid/High
38	Left	Reverse Palm Strik	Front	High
39	Right	Inward Inner Forearm Block	Closed	Low
40	Left	Horizontal Back Elbow Strike	Middle	Middle
41*	Left	Knifehand Strike	Middle	High
42	L/R	Knifehand X-Block	Closed	High
43	Left	Knifehand Strike	Closed	High
44	Left	Knee Strike		Middle
45	Right	Ridgehand Block	Rear	High
46	Right	Horizontal Spearhand	Rear	High
47	Right	Step Spin Hook Kick		Mid/High
48	Left	Low Block	Middle	Low
49	Left	Inner Forearm Block	Middle	High
50	Left	Punch	Middle	Middle
51	Left	Concentration #3 Side Kick		Low
52	Left	Round Kick		Middle
53	Left	Round Kick		Mid/High
54	Left	Dbl Low Block (L- knifehand, R-fist)	Sparring	Low
55	Left	Square Block (R-fist, L-knifehand)	Back	High
56	Left	Upset Knifehand Strike	Back	High
57	Right	Reverse Vertical Punch	Front	Middle
58	Left	#3 Jump Front Kick		Mid/High
59	Right	Reverse Palmheel Strike	Front	High
60	Left	Inward Inner forearm Block	Closed	Low
61	Right	Horizontal Back Elbow Strike	Middle	Middle
62	Right	Knifehand Strike	Middle	High
63	Left	Knifehand High-Low Block	Closed	High/Low
64	Right	Knifehand High-Low Block	Closed	High/Low

Designated Half of Form

Rev 4.0 - © KarateBuilt L.L.C.

Master Club Curriculum - Forms

Shim Jun (3rd Part)

Step	Side	Technique	Stance	Section
65	Left	Ridgehand Block	Rear	High
66	Left	Horizontal Spearhand	Rear	High
67	Left	Step Spin Hook Kick		Mid/High
68	Right	Low Block	Middle	Low
69	Right	Inner Forearm Block	Middle	High
70	Right	Punch	Middle	Middle
71	Right	Concentration #3 Side Kick		Low
72	Right	Round Kick		Middle
73	Right	Round Kick		Mid/High
74	Right	Dbl Low Block (L-fist, R-knifehand)	Sparring	Low
75	Right	Step Forward, #2 Jump Side Kick		Low
76	Right	Advanced Dbl Outer Forearm Block	Back	High
77	Left	Reverse Punch	Back	Middle
78	Right	Low Circle Dbl Outer Forearm Block	Back	Low
79	Left	Advance Dbl Outer Forearm Block	Back	High
80	Right	Reverse Punch	Back	Middle
81	Left	Low Circle Dbl Outer Forearm Block	Back	Low

Rev 4.0 - © KarateBuilt L.L.C.

Master Club Curriculum - Breaks

Name: _____

Graduation Date: __/__/__

Board Break Requirements: 1° Black Belt Decided

Rotation A, D (March Graduations)
Upset Knifehand, Jump Reverse Side Kick

Rotation B, E (July Graduations)
Knifehand, Jump Side Kick (2 Obstacles*)

Rotation C, F (November Graduations)
Front Kick, Side Kick, Round Kick (One must be done with other foot)

Board Color Guidelines
The color of board required is listed below. This is only a guide, however and students may be asked to break lighter or heavier boards based on instructor recommendation.

Age	Color	Age	Color
Under 7	White	11-12	Green
7-8	Yellow	13-15	Blue
9-10	Orange	16+ Female	Blue
		16+ Male	Brown

*Obstacle requirements are based on student size, age and rank.

Rev 4.0 - © KarateBuilt L.L.C.

My Notes on My Road to Master

Master Club Curriculum - SJB

Ssahng Jeol Bong Combat Drills
(Note that all of these drills and strikes must be adjusted to compensate for the attacking angle. Starts with attacker in sparring stance, defender in parallel stance. Only #1-#6 required for kids midterming or testing))

Line #1 Strike
Step Back with Left; Block with Triangle; Horizontal Twirl.

Line #2 Strike
Step Forward with Left; High/Low Block (push partner's hand put of the way); V-Strike; Double Hand V-Strike.

Line #3 Strike
Step Forward with Right; High/Low Block; Double Step Back; Under-Arm X-Strike (switching hands); Under-Arm X-Strike; High/Low Block; High/Low Block; Tip X-Strike (strike with tip of SJB).

Line #4 Strike
Step Back with Left; Triangle; Lasso (behind back); Front Neck Circle.

Line #5 Strike
Step Back with Left; Low Triangle; Leg Strike (right leg); SJB Goes Behind Back, Around Left Foot, Kick up Gently to Left Hand (catch in inverted position); Lasso (behind the back).

Line #6 Strike (Last Required for Kid Black Belt Testing)
Step Back with Right; Left Triangle; Hand Over (over the shoulder); Left Triangle.

Line #7 Strike
Step Back with Right; Straight Block, Tip X-Strike(strike with tip of SJB); Strike with Double End of SJB.

Line #8 Strike
Step Forward with Left; High/Low Block; End Strike (right end); End Strike (left end); Tip X-Strike(strike with tip of SJB).

Line #9 Strike
Step Back with Right; Straight Block; Disarm by Crossing String Around

Single Ssahng Jeol Bong Form

Your form is on the following pages. These are reprinted by permission of the American Taekwondo Association

The pattern of the form is as follows:

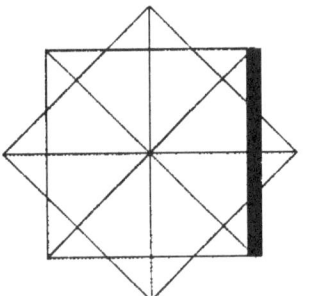

Master Club Curriculum - SJB

Single Ssahng Jeol Bong Form

		Technique		Stance
1.	R	High/Low Ready Position		R Back
2.	R	#1 Angle Strike	w/L Forward Shuffle	R Back
3.	R	Waist Swing		R Back
4.	R	Upwards Spin		R Back
5.	R	One Hand Ready Position		R Back
6.	R	#1 Angle Strike	w/L Forward Shuffle	R Back
7.	R	Waist Swing		R Back
8.	R	Upwards Spin		R Back
9.	R	One Hand Ready Position		R Back
10.	R	#1 Angle Strike	w/L Forward Shuffle	R Back
11.	R	Waist Swing		R Back
12.	R	Upwards Spin		R Back
13.	R	One Hand Ready Position		R Back
14.	R	#1 Angle Strike		R Back
15.	R	360° Horizontal Twirl		R Back
16.	R	Waist Swing		R Back
17.	R	Upwards Spin		R Back
18.	R	One Hand Ready Position		R Back
19.	R	"V" Strike	w/L Forward Shuffle	R Back
20.	R	Upwards Spin		R Back
21.	R	One Hand Ready Position		R Back
22.	R	Waist Swing		R Back
23.	R	Behind Back Hand Switch		R Back
24.	R	Behind Neck Switch		R Back
25.	R	Upwards Spin		R Back
26.	R	One Hand Ready Position		R Back
27.	R	Under Arm Swing		R Back
28.	R	Waist Swing		R Back
29.	R	Upwards Spin		R Back
30.	R	One Hand Ready Position		R Back
31.	R	Step Through with Propeller Strike		R Back
32.	R	Waist Swing		R Back
33.	R	Upwards Spin		R Back
34.	R	High/Low Ready Position		R Back

Rev 4.0 - © KarateBuilt L.L.C.

Single Ssahng Jeol Bong Form (Part 2)

35.	L	Step Through w/ High/Low Ready Position	R Back
36.	R/L	Under Arm "X" Strike	R Back
37.	L	High/Low Ready Position	R Back
38.	L	#1 Angle Strike	R Back
39.	L	Waist Swing	R Back
40.	L	Upwards Spin	R Back
41.	L	One Hand Ready Position	R Back
42.	L	#1 Angle Strike	L Back
43.	L	Waist Swing	L Back
44.	L	Upwards Spin	L Back
45.	L	One Hand Ready Position	L Back
46.	L	#1 Angle Strike w/R Forward Shuffle	L Back
47.	L	Waist Swing	L Back
48.	L	Upwards Spin	L Back
49.	L	One Hand Ready Position	L Back
50.	L	#1 Angle Strike w/R Forward Shuffle	L Back
51.	L	Waist Swing	L Back
52.	L	Upwards Spin	L Back
53.	L	One Hand Ready Position	L Back
54.	L	#1 Angle Strike	L Back
55.	L	360° Horizontal Twirl	L Back
56.	L	Waist Swing	L Back
57.	L	Upwards Spin	L Back
58.	L	One Hand Fighting Position	L Back
59.	L	"V" Strike w/R Forward Shuffle	L Back
60	L	Upwards Spin	L Back
61.	R	One Hand Ready Position	L Back
62.	L	Waist Swing	L Back
63.	L	Behind Back Hand Switch	L Back
64.	L	Behind Neck Switch	L Back
65.	L	Upwards Spin	L Back
66.	L	One hand Ready Position	L Back
67.	L	Under Arm Swing	L Back
68.	L	Waist Swing	L Back

Single Ssahng Jeol Bong Form (Part 3)

69.	L	Upwards Spin	L Back
70.	R	One Hand Ready Position	L Back
71.	L	Step Through with Propeller Strike	L Back
72.	L	Waist Swing	L Back
73.	L	Upwards Spin	L Back
74.	L	High/Low Ready Position	L Back
75.	R	Step Through w/ High/Low Ready Position	L Back
76.	L/R	Under Arm "X" Strike	L Back
77.	R	High/Low Ready Position	L Back
78.	R	#1 Angle Strike	L Back
79.	R	Waist Swing	L Back
80.	R	Upwards Spin	L Back
81.	R	One Hand Ready Position	L Back
82.	R	#1 Angle Strike	R Back
83.	R	Waist Swing	R Back
84.	R	Upwards Spin	R Back
85.	R	One Hand Ready Position	R Back

Master Club Curriculum - BME

Bahng Mahng Ee Combat Drills

(Note that all of these drills and strikes must be adjusted to compensate for the attacking angle. Starts with attacker in sparring stance, defender in parallel stance. All finish with twirl to defensive position)

Line #1 Strike
Step Back with Left; Block with Reinforced #1 Strike (Basic Block); #1 Strike to Hand; #2 Strike to Neck; #3 Strike to Kidney; #4 Strike to Kidney.

Line #2 Strike
Step Forward with Left; Block with Reinforced #2 (Basic Block); Left Hand Disarm; Heel Strike to Elbow; Round Kick; Double Horizontal Fan.

Line #3 Strike
Step Back with Left; #3 Basic Block; Left Hand Disarm; Right Foot Steps to Right, #1 Strike to Neck (Striking Through); #4 Strike to Neck; Right Leg Side Kick.

Line #4 Strike
Step Forward with Left; Block with Reinforced #2 (Basic Block); Strike Hand; Disarm with Stick; #1 Strike; #9 Strike to Throat.

Line #5 Strike
Step Back With Left; Pass Stick to Right with Left Hand, #1 Strike to Forearm; Slide Stick Across to #2 Strike to Neck; #6 Strike to Knee; Double Horizontal Fan; Double Vertical Fan.

Line #6 Strike (Last Required for Kid Black Belt Testing)
Jump Over Stick, Passing with #5 Strike; #2 Strike to Neck; #2 Strike to Arm; #2 Strike to Head; Stick Between Legs & Pull Up to Groin; Pull Out with Left Hand; #1 Strike to Back of Head.

Line #7 Strike
Step Back with Right; 2 Handed, Straight Block, Rake Hands to Left; Right Round Kick; Double Horizontal Fan; Double Vertical Fan.

Line #8 Strike
Step Back with Right; High Block; Push Hand Away; #1 Strike to Forearm; Switch to Left Hand; #1 Strike to Neck; #2 to Neck.

Line #9 Strike
Step Back with Right; Tip Down Block Across; Circle Arm to #7 Strike to Groin; Twirl to #8 Strike to Head; Heel Strike to Head.

Master Club Curriculum - BME

Name: _____

Graduation Date: __/__/__

Single Bahng Mahng Ee Form

Your form is on the following pages. These are reprinted by permission of the American Taekwondo Association

The pattern of the form is as follows:

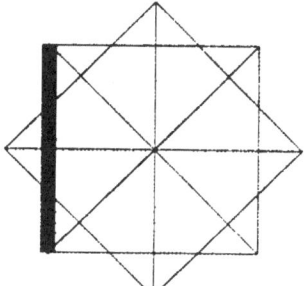

Rev 4.0 - © KarateBuilt L.L.C.

Master Club Curriculum - BME

Single Bahng Mahng Ee Form (Part 1)

Description of:
Bahng Mahng Ee Fighting Stance
  Wider than Taekwondo Sparring Stance, Both knees bent,
  Front foot flat -
  Back foot heel is slightly off the floor
Uneven Middle Stance
  Same width and feet position as Taekwondo Middle Stance
  70% of weight on leg that steps into the stance
Attention (facing East)
Bow
June Bee! (Right foot steps - holding Bahng Mahng Ee in both hands, in front of body, parallel to floor)

1. Right foot steps back (toward West) to Right Back Stance (facing East) right hand twisting strike
2. Move Left foot left to Left Bahng Mahng Ee Fighting Stance; #1 Angle Strike, Right foot pivots
3. Shift weight back to Right Back Stance; #2 Angle Strike, Left foot pivots
4. Shift weight again to Left Bahng Mahng Ee Fighting Stance; #3 Angle Strike, right foot pivots
5. Shift weight back to Right Back Stance; #4 Angle Strike, Left foot pivots
6. Turning clockwise 180, Right foot steps to Right Bahng Mahng Ee Fighting Stance (facing West); #6 Angle Backhand Strike
7. Left foot steps forward (West) to Left Bahng Mahng Ee Fighting Stance, over head #5 Angle Strike
8. Right foot slides to Right Back Stance; #2 Angle Slash (slow)
9. Turning clockwise 180, Right foot steps to Left Back Stance (facing East); #9 Angle Butt Strike to Target and in continuous motion Fighting Stance
10. #1 Angle Strike with "pull through" in place
11. High Fan Strike (counterclockwise) and in continuous motion
12. High Fan Strike (clockwise) with pull through and in continuous motion
13. Pull Right Foot back into Left Rear Stance; #1 Angle Strike with "pull through"
14. Left foot steps forward (East) to Right Back Stance; #2 Cutting Strike (slow)
15. Step Right Foot diagonally towards South-East into a Right Front Stance Chamber for #1 Angle Power Strike with slight hesitation Shift weight and feet into Left Front Stance; #1 Angle Power Strike Kihap
16. #4 Angle Backhand Strike (slow), Left Front Stance, Right Foot step Left, feet together
17. Step Left foot forward to an uneven middle stance, Right Outside Deflection, In place
18. Right hand Target Strike ***(KIHAP) In place
19. Pull Left foot to Right Rear Stance; Low Outside sweep (Left hand open, palm up)
20. Left foot steps to Left Bahng Mahng Ee Fighting Stance (to East on East-West line) 360 Disarming Technique and in continuous motion...

Single Bahng Mahng Ee Form (Part 2)

21. Butt Strike to Target
22. #2 Right Round Kick (to East), Land Right foot forward Right Fighting Stance
23. High Fan Strike (counterclockwise) and in continuous motion...
24. High Fan Strike (clockwise) with pull through and in continuous motion...
25. #1 Angle Strike with "pull-through" In place Left Rear Stance
26. Low Fan Strike (clockwise) and in continuous motion
27. Low Fan Strike (counterclockwise) with 360 twirl up to Right shoulder; Stepping Left Foot to Right Back Stance
28. 360 Vertical Twirl down into #8 Cutting Strike
29. Step Left Foot back to Right Bahng Mahng Ee Fighting Stance; Left Hand Low Deflecting Technique and in continuous motion...
30. Pull Right Foot back to Left Rear Stance; Low Target Strike
31. Step Left Foot to South-East into an Uneven Middle Stance; Right Outside Deflection In place
32. Right Hand Target Strike, Pull back
33. Digging Disarm (beginning); Pull Left Foot back to Right Rear Stance
34. Digging Disarm (completion)
35. Step Left Foot into Left Bahng Mahng Ee Fighting Stance; #1 Angle Power Cutting Strike ***(KIHAP) in continuous motion... #9 Thrust Cross Stance
36. Turn 180 clockwise, stepping Right Foot into Right Bahng Mahng Ee Fighting Stance (facing west)
37. High Fan Strike (counterclockwise) and in continuous motion...
38. High Fan Strike (clockwise) and in continuous motion...
39. Pull Right Foot back into Left Rear Stance; #1 Angle Strike with "pull-through"
40. Double step forward (shuffle) into Right Bahng Mahng Ee Fighting Stance; High Fan Strike (counterclockwise) and in continuous motion...
41. High Fan Strike (clockwise) and in continuous motion...
42. Pull Right Foot back into Left Rear Stance; #1 Angle Strike with "pull-through"
43. Step Right Foot forward to Right Front Stance; High Block with Left Hand Deflection In place
44. #1 Angle Strike
45. Switch weapon hand (right to left) in slow motion (motion similar to sheathing a sword)
46. Pull Right Foot back to Left Back Stance

(With the weapon now in the left hand)

47. Move Right foot right to Right Bahng Mahng Ee Fighting Stance; #1 Angle Strike, Left foot pivots
48. Shift weight back to Left Back Stance; #2 Angle Strike, Right foot pivots
49. Shift weight again to Right Bahng Mahng Ee Fighting Stance; #3 Angle Strike, left foot pivots
50. Shift weight back to Left Back Stance; #4 Angle Strike, Right foot pivots

Rev 4.0 - © KarateBuilt L.L.C.

Master Club Curriculum - BME

Single Bahng Mahng Ee Form (Part 3)

51. Turning counterclockwise 180, Left foot steps to Left Bahng Mahng Ee Fighting Stance (facing East); #6 Angle Backhand Strike
52. Right foot steps forward (East) to Right Bahng Mahng Ee Fighting Stance, over head #5 Angle Strike
53. Left foot slides to Left Back Stance; #2 Angle Slash (slow)
54. Turning counterclockwise 180, Left foot steps to Right Back Stance (facing West); #9 Angle Butt Strike to Target and in continuous motion Fighting Stance
55. #1 Angle Strike with "pull through" in place
56. High Fan Strike (clockwise) and in continuous motion
57. High Fan Strike (counterclockwise) with pull through and in continuous motion
58. Pull Left Foot back into Right Rear Stance; #1 Angle Strike with "pull through"
59. Right foot steps forward (West) to Left Back Stance; #2 Cutting Strike (slow)
60. Step Left Foot diagonally towards North-West into a Left Front Stance Chamber for #1 Angle Power Strike with slight hesitation Shift weight and feet into Right Front Stance; #1 Angle Power Strike
61. #4 Angle Backhand Strike (slow), Right Front Stance, Left Foot step Right, feet together
62. Step Right foot forward to an uneven middle stance, Left Outside Deflection, In place
63. Left hand Target Strike ***(KIHAP) In place
64. Pull Right foot to Left Rear Stance; Low Outside sweep (Right hand open, palm up)
65. Right foot steps to Right Bahng Mahng Ee Fighting Stance (to West on East-West line) 360 Disarming Technique and in continuous motion...
66. Butt Strike to Target
67. #2 Left Round Kick (to West), Land Left foot forward Left Fighting Stance
68. High Fan Strike (clockwise) and in continuous motion...
69. High Fan Strike (counterclockwise) with pull through and in continuous motion...
70. #1 Angle Strike with "pull-through" In place Right Rear Stance
71. Low Fan Strike (counterclockwise) and in continuous motion
72. Low Fan Strike (clockwise) with 360 twirl up to Left shoulder; Stepping Right Foot to Left Back Stance
73. 360 Vertical Twirl down into #8 Cutting Strike
74. Step Right Foot back to Left Bahng Mahng Ee Fighting Stance; Right Hand Low Deflecting Technique and in continuous motion...
75. Pull Left Foot back to Right Rear Stance; Low Target Strike
76. Step Right Foot to North-West into an Uneven Middle Stance; Left Outside Deflection In place
77. Left Hand Target Strike, Pull back
78. Digging Disarm (beginning); Pull Right Foot back to Left Rear Stance
79. Digging Disarm (completion)
80. Step Right Foot into Right Bahng Mahng Ee Fighting Stance; #1 Angle Power Cutting Strike ***(KIHAP) in continuous motion... #9 Thrust Cross Stance
81. Turn 180 counterclockwise, stepping Left Foot into Left Bahng Mahng Ee Fighting Stance (facing east)

REV 4.0 - © KarateBuilt L.L.C.

Single Bahng Mahng Ee Form (Part 4)

82. High Fan Strike (clockwise) and in continuous motion...
83. High Fan Strike (counterclockwise) and in continuous motion...
84. Pull Left Foot back into Right Rear Stance; #1 Angle Strike with "pull-through"
85. Double step forward (shuffle) into Left Bahng Mahng Ee Fighting Stance; High Fan Strike (clockwise) and in continuous motion...
86. High Fan Strike (counterclockwise) and in continuous motion...
87. Pull Left Foot back into Right Rear Stance; #1 Angle Strike with "pull-through"
88. Step Left Foot forward to Left Front Stance; High Block with Right Hand Deflection In place
89. #1 Angle Strike
90. Right Foot forward Ready Position

Right Foot to Left — Bahro with Bahng Mahng Ee in left hand — Shuit!

My Notes on My Road to Master

2°R Black Belt to 2°D Black Belt Rank Requirements:

This is a very important time on your road to mastery. This is when you are challenged by the transition to 2° Black Belt. This is a high rank in Taekwondo. You have to keep building your skills to handle the coordination, focus and balance required by 2° Black Belt curriculum. Plus, more complicated forms, and more difficult board breaks. To prepare for this, midterms require special Combat Drills review of lower rank material, Shim Jun, and new board breaks. Good luck continuing on your "Road to Mastery"!

My Notes on My Road to Master

Master Club

2° Black Belt Curriculum

2° Black Belt to 3° Black Belt Rank Requirements:

Congratulations! You are now a 2nd Degree Decided Black Belt! Take a few moments and fill out the "Road to Mastery" planner on the next page. It is important to focus on your training and continue to set goals. This helps you continue to grow and get stronger in martial arts - both mentally and physically. At this stage more will be asked of you and you will have greater responsibility both at the martial arts school and at home with your family. This will be an awesome time for you - the time to step toward Mastery in Taekwondo!

My Road to Mastery!

3° Black Belt Planner:

Take a minute and plan your road to 3° black belt.
Your instructor can help you find the correct dates.
At 2°, you should plan on midterming every 4 months and you will need required ProTech Equipment (see ProTech Rotation).

Current Rank	Testing For:	Requirements:	Graduation Fee:*	My Test Date
1° D	2°R	Instructor Permission, 1 Year at Rank, Shim Jun, Sparring, Board Breaks **at Graduation**, Currrent ProTech Basics or Whole Current ProTech Form	$80	__/__/__
2° R	Midterm	Instructor Permission, 2 Months at Rank, Shim Jun, New Board Breaks, Current 2°R ProTech Requirements	$80	__/__/__
2° R	2°D	Instructor Permission, 4 Months at Rank, Shim Jun, New Board Breaks **at Graduation**, Sparring, Current 2°R ProTech Requirements	$80	__/__/__
2°D	Midterm#1	Instructor Permission, 4 Months at Rank, 1/2 Jung Yul, Current 2° ProTech Basics 1/2 Current 2° ProTech Form/Flow	$80	__/__/__
2°D	Midterm#2	Instructor Permission, 8 Months at Rank, Jung Yul, Sparring, 1/2 Current 2° ProTech Form/Flow	$80	__/__/__
2°D	Midterm#3	Instructor Permission, 1 Year at Rank, 1/2 Current 2° ProTech Form/Flow	$80	__/__/__
2°D	Midterm#4	Instructor Permission, 16 Months at Rank, Jung Yul, Board Breaks, Current 2° ProTech Form/Flow	$80	__/__/__
2°D	Midterm#5	Instructor Permission, 20 Months at Rank, Sparring Current 2° ProTech Form/Flow	$80	__/__/__
2°D	Midterm#6	Instructor Permission, 2 Years at Rank, Jung Yul, Board Breaks, Current 2° ProTech Form/Flow	$80	__/__/__
2°D	3°D	Instructor Permission, 28 Months at Rank, Jung Yul, Board Breaks **at Graduation**, Sparring, All 2° ProTech Requirements	$80	__/__/__

*Graduation fees and requirements subject to change.

Rev 4.0 - © KarateBuilt L.L.C.

Master Club 2° Black Belt
ProTech Material Rotation

March Graduation	July Graduation	November Graduation
Ssahng Nat Form	Double Ssahng Jeol Bong Form	Double Bahng Mahng Ee Form

Required Equipment*

Korean Name	Common Name	Abbreviation	Required
Ssahng Jeol Bong	Nunchaku	SJB	Two Required
Bahng Mahng Ee	Stick	BME	Two Required
Ssahng Nat	Double Kama	SN	Two Required

* For your safety, all equipment must be American Taekwondo Association / ProTech approved

Name: _____

Graduation Date: __/__/__

Jung Yul
"With Your Noble Character, You Will Develop a New Permanence in Your Life"

Your form is on the following pages. These are reprinted by permission of the American Taekwondo Association

The pattern of the form is as follows:

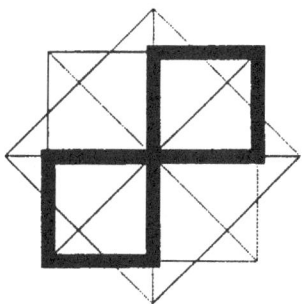

Master Club Curriculum - Forms

Jung Yul (Part 1)

1.	L	Horizontal Elbow; R-Vertical Back Elbow	M	M&H
2.	L	Square Block	M	H
3.	R	Horizontal Elbow; L-Vertical Back Elbow	M	M&H
4.	R	Square Block	M	H
5.	B	Twin Punch	C	H
6.	R	Punch	X	H
7.	R	Downward Elbow Strike	X	L
8.	R	Circular Double Knifehand Low Block	X	L
9.	L	Reverse Hooking Block	F	H
10.	R	Hooking Block	F	H
11.	L	Reverse Vertical Punch	F	H
12.	L	#2 Ax Kick	--	H
13.	L	Knifehand Low Block	F	L
14.	R	Circular Reverse Knifehand Block	F	H
15.	L	Arc Hand Strike	OL	H
16.	R	Upward Elbow	OL	H
17.	B	Knifehand & Open Hand Block	OL	H&L
18.	R	Reinforced Inner Forearm Block	X	H
19.	R	Back Fist	X	H
20.	R	Horizontal Hammer Fist	X	H
21.	R	Circular Double knifehand Block	B	H
22.	L	#2 Inner Crescent Kick - Ki-hap	--	H
23.	R	Reverse Hook Kick	--	H
24.	R	Round Kick	--	H
25.	R	High Block	B	H
26.	R	Downward Palm Block	R	L
27.	R	Punch	M	H
28.	R	Inward Palm Block	B	M
29.	L	Reverse Punch	B	H
30.	R	Upset Knifehand Strike	B	H
31.	R	Circular Downward Knifehand Strike	X	H
32.	R	#2 Front Kick	--	H
33.	R	#1 Side Kick	--	H
34.	R	Circular Double Outer Forearm Low Block	M	L
35.	L	Circular Double Knifehand Block	B	H
36.	R	#2 Round Kick	--	H
37.	R	Round Kick	--	H
38.	R	Round Kick		H

Jung Yul (Part 2)

39.	R	Downward Double Knifehand Strike	S	H
40.	B	High Nine Block	R	H&L
41.	L	Downward Double Knifehand Strike	S	H
42.	B	High Nine Block - Ki-hap	R	H&L
43.	R	Butterfly Kick	--	H
44.	L	Reverse Side Kick	--	M/H
45.	R	#2 Side Kick	--	M/H
46.	R	Downward Double Knifehand Strike	S	H
47.	L	#2 Round Kick	--	H
48.	L	Round Kick	--	H
49.	L	Round Kick	--	H
50.	B	Twin Punch	C	H
51.	L	Punch	X	H
52.	L	Downward Elbow Strike	X	L
53.	L	Circular Double Knifehand Low Block	X	L
54.	R	Reverse Hooking Block	F	H
55.	L	Hooking Block	F	H
56.	R	Reverse Vertical Punch	F	H
57.	R	#2 Ax Kick	--	H
58.	R	Knifehand Low Block	F	L
59.	L	Circular Reverse Knifehand Block	F	H
60.	R	Arc Hand Strike	OL	H
61.	L	Upward Elbow	OL	H
62.	B	Knifehand & Open Hand Block - Ki-hap	OL	H&L
63.	L	Reinforced Inner Forearm Block	X	H
64.	L	Back Fist	X	H
65.	L	Horizontal Hammer Fist	X	H
66.	L	Circular Double Knifehand Block	B	H
67.	R	#2 Inner Crescent Kick	--	H
68.	L	Reverse Hook Kick	--	H
69.	L	Round Kick	--	H
70.	L	High Block	B	H
71.	L	Downward Palm Block	R	L
72.	L	Punch	M	H
73.	L	Inward Palm Block	B	M
74.	R	Reverse Punch	B	H
75.	L	Upset Knifehand Strike	B	H
76.	L	Circular Downward Knifehand Strike	X	H

Rev 4.0 - © KarateBuilt L.L.C.

Master Club Curriculum - Forms

Jung Yul (Part 3)

77.	L	#2 Front Kick	--	H
78.	L	#1 Side Kick	--	H
79.	L	Circular Double Outer Forearm Low Block	M	L
80.	R	Circular Double Knifehand Block	M	L
81.	L	Knifehand Strike	B	H
82.	R	Reverse Punch	B	H

Master Club Curriculum - Breaks

Name: _____

Graduation Date: __/__/__

Board Break Requirements: 2° Black Belt Decided

Rotation A (March Graduations)
Hammerfist, #3 Jump Axe Kick (Face Level)

Rotation B (July Graduations)
Upset Hammerfist, #2 Jump Round Kick (Face Level)

Rotation C (November Graduations)
Backfist, Side Kick/Round Kick (Continuous Kick With Same Foot, Not Letting It Touch The Floor)

Alternate
Step Forward Spin Hook Kick, Jump Side Kick (2 Obstacles)

Board Color Guidelines

The color of board required is listed below. This is only a guide, however and students may be asked to break lighter or heavier boards based on instructor recommendation.

Age	Color	Age	Color
Under 7	White	11-12	Green
7-8	Yellow	13-15	Blue
9-10	Orange	16+ Female	Blue
		16+ Male	Brown

*Obstacle requirements are based on student size, age and rank.

Rev 4.0 - © KarateBuilt L.L.C.

My Notes on My Road to Master

Double Ssahng Jeol Bong Drills

The Double Ssahng Jeol Bong drills are on the following pages. At graduation 1° Black Belts are required to know all of these, and perform a freestyle of at least 30 seconds made up of these drills. These are reprinted by permission of the American Taekwondo Association

Double Ssahng Jeol Bong Drills

Drill #1 - Feet Apart
Step out and simultaneously strike downward, hitting SJB on inner leg.

Drill #2 - Feet Together
Strike downward, hitting SJB on armpits and back to tricep.

Drill #3 - Feet Apart
Step sut and simultaneously put both SJB together, strike downward, hitting SJB on inner leg/buttocks, then back up to the Left shoulder area, back to the inner leg/buttocks, then to the right shoulder area, then twirl back up to a high load position..

Drill #4 - Feet Apart
Step out and simultaneously strike downward, hitting SJB on inner leg; inward twirl, outward twirl; bring hands up to shoulder in high load position; strike downward again; three inward twirls and simultaneously step together; finish with a drill #2.

Drill #5 - Feet Together
Strike downward, alternatingly hitting SJB on armpits and back to tricep.

Drill #6 - Feet Together
Strike downward, alternatingly hitting left SJB on armpits and back to tricep, while right SJB hits across to left hip and back to tricep.

Drill #7 - Feet Apart (in Shoulder Width Stance)
Triangles without upwards twirl. One SJB strikes across to opposite hip, back across belly to same side hip and then up to tricep; as first SJB moves from same side hip to tricep, other SJB strikes to opposite hip, and follows back across belly to same side hip, and back to tricep (repeating sequence).

Drill #8 - Feet Apart
Step out and simultaneously strike downward with right SJB; alternate with left, then right again; step together and continuously alternate left, right left strikes (landing on tricep.

Drill #9 - Feet Apart (in Shoulder Width Stance)
Same as number 7, except right SJB twirls horizontally over the head before striking opposite hip.

Double Ssahng Jeol Bong Form

Your form is on the following pages. These are reprinted by permission of the American Taekwondo Association

The pattern of the form is as follows:

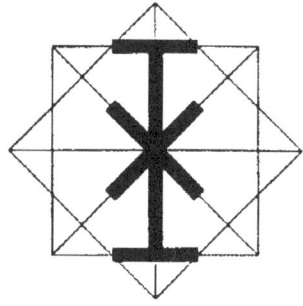

Master Club Curriculum - DSJB

Double Ssahng Jeol Bong Form (Part 1)

Start: Begin by facing east.
Attention: Feet together, with one Ssahng Jeol Bong in each hand. Bow.
June Bee: Step to the left with left foot, feet shoulder width apart. Both hands to upper shoulder ready position.

Segment 1
1. Right foot 1/2 steps back to southwest while executing a right triangle swing.

2. Left foot single steps to southeast while executing a right hand triangle swing, left hand triangle swing.

3. Right foot single steps southeast while executing a right hand triangle swing, left hand triangle swing.

4. Right foot steps back to center while executing a right hand triangle swing. Changing directions.

Segment 2
5. Left foot steps to southwest while executing a left hand triangle swing.

6. Right foot single steps forward while executing a right #9 double Ssahng Jeol Bong drill.

7. Right foot single steps back to center while executing a #9 drill changing into #7 right hand high/left hand low position.

Segment 3
8. Left foot single steps to northwest while executing a #7 drill.

9. Right foot single steps forward while executing a #5 drill 2-3 times.

10. Right foot single steps back to center while executing a #5 drill 2-3 times.

11. No step, execute a #6 drill 3-4 times on the right hand side.

Segment 4
12. Left foot single steps to the northeast while executing a #7 drill with right hand high/left hand low position.

13. Right foot single steps forward while executing a #6 drill with right hand high/left hand low position.

14. No step, left hand side #6 drill.

160   REV 4.0 - © KarateBuilt L.L.C.

Double Ssahng Jeol Bong Form (Part 2)

15. Right foot single steps back to center while executing a right triangle swing, one spin up with both Ssahng Jeol Bongs to upper shoulder position.

16. No step. With left hand remaining at upper shoulder position execute a right hand diagonal strike.

17. 360 degree horizontal twirl clockwise.

18. No step. Right hand diagonal strike.

19. 360 degree horizontal twirl counterclockwise, ending with both hands in the upper shoulder position.

Segment 5
20. Left foot single steps to the East while executing a left triangle drill with one spin up to upper shoulder position.

21. Right foot single steps into a cross stance facing east while executing a right triangle drill with one spin up to upper shoulder position.

22. No step, 360 degree turn.

23. #3 left jump front kick landing in a right back stance.

Segment 6
24. Right foot steps forward into a middle stance facing east.

25. Execute a #1 drill 3-4 times.

Segment 7
26. Double step to left into a middle stance facing east.

27. Execute a #1 drill 3-4 times.

28. End with the left foot stepping to right foot in a closed stance facing east with both Ssahng Jeol Bongs ending in the upper shoulder position.

Segment 8
29. Right foot steps out into a middle stance facing east while...

30. Execute a right hand #8 drill.

31. Right foot steps to left facing east in a closed stance while executing a right high/ left hand low.

Double Ssahng Jeol Bong Form (Part 3)

32. Left foot steps left into a middle stance while executing a right hand #8 drill.

33. Left foot steps back to a closed stance facing east. Right hand high/left hand low to kidney area and execute a #8 drill.

34. Execute a #5 drill 2-3 times.

Segment 9
35. Left foot steps back toward the west, (still facing east) while executing one #5 drill with left hand high/right hand low.

36. Right foot steps back toward west, (still facing east) while executing one #5 drill with right hand high/left hand low.

37. Left foot steps back toward west, (still facing east) while executing one #5 drill.

38. End with a right hand #2 drill 3-4 times.

39. Right foot single steps back facing the west.

40. Execute a right hand triangle drill with one spin up to the upper shoulder position.

41. Left foot single steps forward into a cross stance.

42. Execute a left hand triangle drill.

Segment 10
43. No step 360 degree turn.

44. #3 right jump front kick landing in a left back stance.

45. Left foot steps forward into a middle stance facing west.

46. #1 drill 3-4 times.

Segment 11
47. Double step to the right into a middle stance while facing west.

48. Execute a #1 drill 3-4 times.

49. Right foot steps to the left into a closed stance while facing west with both Ssahng Jeol Bongs in the upper shoulder position.

Double Ssahng Jeol Bong Form (Part 4)

Segment 12

50. Left foot steps out into a middle stance facing west.

51. While executing a left hand #8 drill.

52. Left foot steps to right facing west in a closed stance while executing a left high/right hand low #5 drill.

53. Right foot steps right into a middle stance while executing a left hand #8 drill.

54. Left foot steps back to a closed stance facing west with left hand high/ right hand low and execute a #8 drill.

Segment 13

55. Execute a #5 drill 2-3 times.

56. Right foot steps back toward east (while facing west) executing a #5 drill with right hand high/ left hand low to kidney area.

57. Right foot triple steps back toward center (facing west) while executing a #5 drill with left hand high/ right hand low.

58. Left foot steps back toward east (facing west) executing a #5 drill 3-4 times.

59. End with a left hand #2 drill 2-3 times.

60. Left foot single steps back turning 180 degrees facing east.

61. While executing a left hand triangle drill with one spin up to the upper shoulder position.

62. Right foot single steps forward into a middle stance.

63. While executing a #1 drill 3-4 times.

64. #3 drill 3-4 times.

65. #4 drill 3-4 times.

66. Double cross waist swing 2 times.

67. Double armpit grab.

Bahro

My Notes on My Road to Master

Double Bahng Mahng Ee Drills

The Double Bahng Mahng Ee drills are on the following pages. At graduation 1° Black Belts are required to know all of these, and perform a freestyle of at least 30 seconds made up of these drills. These are reprinted by permission of the American Taekwondo Association

Double Bahng Mahng Ee Warm Up Drills

Basic	Description
1	Double X
2	Umbrella 2 Circles - cut
3	Figure 8
4	Reverse Figure 8
5	Figure 8 Down Strike
6	Propeller
7	Praying 6 Count
8	Reverse Wipe
9	High Block Down Strike

Double Bahng Mahng Ee Positions

Position	Description
1	High Open
2	Low Open
3	High Closed
4	High / Low Closed
5	High / Low Open

Double Bahng Mahng Ee Level 1 Drills

Basic   **Description**

1   **Double Cross Strike**
Start in High/Low Closed position, lower BME Strikes across first, followed by upper (switching sides and positions)

2   **Defensive 3 Count (6 Count)**
Start in High/Low Closed position, lower BME Strikes first (blocking opponent BME), followed by upper BME (striking the opponent hand), followed by first BME striking opponent. Finish in opposite High/Low Closed position.

3   **3 Count (6 Count)**
Start in High/Low Closed position, upper BME Strikes first, followed by lower BME, followed by first BME striking opponent. Finish in opposite High/Low Closed position.

4   **Figure 8**
Crossing in opposite directions.

5   **Double Strike Across**
Start in High Open position, strike one Line 1, Other Line 4 (opposite directions) finish with both across body.

6   **"C" Strike**
Start in High Open position, one BME strikes Line 1, Line 6 (head, knee), other does the mirrored strike.

7   **Twirls**
Forward together / Reverse / Opposite Direction.

8   **High Low / Reverse Wipe**
Same as warm up drill.

9   **5 Count**
Start in High/Low Open position, lower BME Strikes, followed by upper BME, first BME crosses over & strikes, second BME strikes (so far all strikes are to the same side) then first BME strikes other side. Finish in opposite High/Low Open position.

Double Bahng Mahng Ee Level 1 Partner Count Drills

<u>Count</u>   <u>Description</u>
- 1   High open position: #1 strikes
- 2   A) High open position: #1, #2 strikes
  B) High open position: #1, #6 strikes
- 3   High open position: #1, #6, #2 strikes
- 4   High open position: #1, #6, #2, #5 strikes
- 5   High open position: Right #1, #6, Left #2, Right #5, Left #3
- 6   Same as praying 6 Count

Master Club Curriculum - DBME

Name: _____

Graduation Date: __/__/__

Double Bahng Mahng Ee Form

Your form is on the following pages. These are reprinted by permission of the American Taekwondo Association

The pattern of the form is as follows:

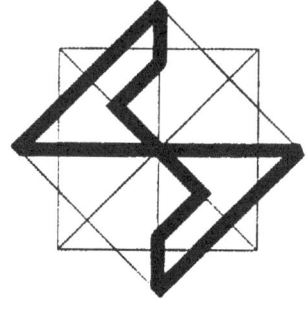

Double Bahng Mahng Ee Form

Begin by facing east with one stick in each hand. Bow. Left foot moves to Jhoon Bee.

Left foot steps to northeast while executing a
1. Palm up/Palm down cutting position

Left foot steps forward while executing a
2. Right low strike
3. Left mid strike
4. Right high strike

Right foot steps forward into a cross stance facing northeast while executing a
5. Left high strike
6. Right low strike

Pivot left 180 degrees to a right back stance facing southeast
7. Right low strike
8. Left mid strike
9. Right high strike

Right foot steps forward into a cross stance facing southeast while executing a
10. Left high strike
11. Right low strike

Left foot steps east into an uneven middle stance while executing a
12. Right high strike
13. Left high strike

Right foot steps forward to east while executing a
14. Right high strike
15. Left high strike
16. Right high strike

Left foot steps forward while executing a
17. Left high strike
18. Right high strike
19. Left high strike

Right foot steps forward while executing a
20. Right high strike
21. Left high strike
22. Right high strike

Double Bahng Mahng Ee Form (Pt 2)

Right foot steps forward while executing a
23. Right high fan strike (striking both left and right directions)
24. Left high strike on right side of the body (striking both left and right directions)
26. Right high strike to left side of the body

Right foot steps across to left facing north while executing a
27. Right low strike

Pivot to the left 180 degrees facing east into a right back stance combat position
28. Left BME strikes Right BME as left foot steps back into the combat position

Right foot steps to left into a cross stance while executing a
29. Right high strike
30. Right low strike

Left foot steps forward into a middle stance while executing a
31. Left high strike
32. Left low strike

Left foot steps back turning 180 degrees into a middle stance while executing a
33. Right high strike
34. Right low strike

Step the right foot to the left foot into a cross stance while executing a
35. Right low strike
36. Left high
37. Left low strike

Turn left 180 degrees facing northwest right foot steps forward into a cross stance while executing a
38. Left low strike
39. Right low strike

Left foot steps forward into a combat drill stance while executing a
40. Double twirl down
41. Double twirl up

Right foot steps to left foot, left foot steps back into a left back stance while executing a
42. Right high strike

Right foot steps back into a right back stance while executing a
43. Left high strike
44. Right high strike

Rev 4.0 - © KarateBuilt L.L.C.

Double Bahng Mahng Ee Form (Pt 3)

Left foot steps back to a left back stance while executing a
45. Left high strike
46. Right high strike
47. Left high strike

Right foot steps across over left foot into a cross stance while executing a
48. Low section double cut

Turn left 180 degrees into a cutting ready stance while
49. Right BME strikes the Left BME

Turn left 180 degrees facing southwest landing in right back stance while executing a
50. Left low drag cut

Right foot steps forward to northwest while executing a
51. High Palm up/Palm down combat ready position

End of the first half

Right foot steps forward while executing a
52.. Left low strike
53. Right mid strike
54. Left high strike

Left foot steps forward into a cross stance facing northwest while executing a
55. Right high strike
56. Left low strike

Pivot 180 degrees to your right landing in a left back stance facing southwest
57. Left low strike
58. Right mid strike
59. Left high strike

Left foot steps forward into a cross stance facing southwest while executing a
60. Right high strike
61. Left low strike

Right foot steps west into an uneven middle stance while executing a
62. Left high strike
63. Right high strike

Double Bahng Mahng Ee Form (Pt 4)

Left foot steps forward facing west while executing a
64. Left high strike
65. Right high strike
66. Left high strike

Right foot steps forward while executing a
67. Right high strike
68. Left high strike
69. Right high strike

Left foot steps forward while executing a
70. Left high strike
71. Right high strike
72. Left high strike

Left foot steps forward while executing a
73. Left high fan strike (striking both right and left directions)
74. Right high strike on left side of the body (striking both right and left directions)
75. Left high strike to right side of body

Left foot steps across to right facing northwest while executing a
76. Left low cutting strike

Pivot right 180 degrees facing northwest into a left back stance combat position
77. Right BME strikes Left BME as right foot steps back into the combat position

Left foot steps to right into a cross stance while executing a
78. Left high strike
79. Left low strike

Right foot steps forward into a middle stance while executing a
80. Right high strike
81. Right low strike

Right foot steps back turning 180 degrees turn into a middle stance while executing a
82. Left high strike

Step the left foot to the right foot into a cross stance while executing a
83. Left low strike
84. Right high strike
    Right low strike

Rev 4.0 - © KarateBuilt L.L.C.

Double Bahng Mahng Ee Form (Pt 5)

Turn right 180 degrees facing southeast left foot steps forward into a cross stance while executing a
85. Right low strike
86. Left low strike

Right foot steps forward to southeast into a combat drill stance while executing a
87. Double twirl down
88. Double twirl up

Left foot steps to right foot, right foot steps back into a right back stance while executing a
89. Left high strike

Left foot steps back into a left back stance while executing a
90. Right high strike
91. Left high strike

Right foot steps back into a right back stance while executing a
92. Right high strike
93. Left high strike
94. Right high strike

No step while facing southeast execute
95. 4 - Figure 8's leading with the right hand
96. Double twirl down
97. Double twirl up
98. Opposite Twirls (right hand twirl forward) while (left hand twirls back)

99. Right foot steps forward. Left foot to bahro

Master Club Curriculum - SN

Name: _____

Graduation Date: __/__/__

Ssahng Nat Form
"Double Kama"

Form Pattern

Starting at the center of the Songahm Star, the numbers represent the technique at the end of that line.

Master Club Curriculum - SN

Ssahng Nat Form
"Double Kama" - Part 1 of 4

Charyut: Right Hand (Holding Both Ssahng Nat) At Side, Left Hand At Side.
June Bee: Closed Stance, Right Hand (Holding Both Ssahng Nat) Up To Waist, Left Hand In Knifehand Low Block Position, Knees Bent.

1. Open Toes Outward. Keeping Knees Bent, Open Heels Outward While Crossing Both Arms In Front With Left Hand On Top Still In Knifehand Position (Palm Down). Right Foot Steps Back To Right Back Stance. Slow Left Knifehand Strike Right Hand Pulls Back As In Horizontal Back Elbow
2. Right Foot Returns To Parallel Stance. Hold Both Ssahng Nat In Front Of Chest; Grip Each Nat In Separate Hand (Ssahng Nat still touching)
3. Big Circle Motion High X Block, Blades Pointing To Sides Until Reaching The Top. In Continuous Motion, Point Blades To Front, Completing The Circle As Right Foot Steps Back In Right Back Stance. Press Down To Side Wing Position
4. Right Hand Figure 8 Stab Back (Behind, Eyes Forward)
5. Cross Hands In Front, Left Horizontal Stab To Left...
6. In Continuos Motion Step Forward With Right Foot, Right Horizontal Stab To Left,
7. Left Foot Steps Back 180 Degrees, Left Stab To Left,
8. Right Stab
9. Continuous Motion Righ't Hand Twirl Down, Turn 180 Degrees To Right, Right Hand Stab
10. Left Hand Stab
11. Right Hand Stab
12. Right Twirl Down With Right Leg Up (1 Leg Stance) (Left foot stays put)
13. Right Foot Lands In Front Stance Facing North With Left Stab
14. Right Hand Multiple High / Low Cuts (4-5 Times)
15. Right Foot Stomps At The Same Time As Right Hand Stab To Right
16. Left Stab
17. Right Foot Steps Back To Closed Stance Facing West, Left Twirl Down To 1 Leg Stance
18. Land In Left Front Stance Facing South, Right Stab
19. Left Hand Multiple High / Low Cuts (4-5 Times)
20. Left Foot Stomps At The Same Time As Left Hand Stab To Left - **Kihap**
21. Right Stab

Ssahng Nat Form
"Double Kama" - Part 2 of 4

22. Left Foot Steps Back To Right Foot, Right Foot Steps Out To Middle Stance Facing South, Twin Parallel Stab.
23. Left Foot Steps Behind To X Stance (Facing Southeast), Horizontal Figure 8 Strike And Stab.
24. Downward Twirl
25. Upward Twirl
26. Twin Stab
27. Downward Twirl And Continuous Motion Right Hand Figure 8 As Left Foot Steps Back To Back Stance (Facing East).
28. Left Stab
29. Right Stab
30. Right Foot Steps Behind To X Stance (Facing Northeast), Horizontal Figure 8 Strike And Stab
31. Downward Twirl
32. Upward Twirl
33. Twin Stab
34. Downward Twirl And Continuous Motion Left Hand Figure 8 As Right Foot Steps Back To Back Stance (Facing East)
35. Right Stab
36. Left Stab
37. Left Foot Steps Back To Parallel Stance, Slow Twin Low Block
38. Large Circle Block, Crossing Hands High & Ending With Natural Ready Stance
39. Left Foot Steps To Right Back Stance Facing North, Double Circular Stab
40. Right Hand Twirl Down & Continuous Circle Motion, Twin Stab. Land In Front Stance
41. Twin Twirl Downward Continuous Upward Twirl
42. Twin High Stab
43. Twirl Figure 8 (Right Hand On Top)
44. Twin Stab With Stomp - **Kihap**

Master Club Curriculum - SN

Ssahng Nat Form
"Double Kama" - Part 3 of 4

45. Double Step Back, Low Stab With Right Hand In Right Back Stance
46. Shift To Left Back Stance Facing South, Double Circular Stab
47. Left Hand Twirl Down & Continuous Circle Motion, Twin Stab. Land In Front Stance
48. Twin Twirl Downward Continuous Upward Twirl
49. Twin High Stab
50. Twirl Figure 8 (Left Hand On Top)
51. Twin Stab With Stomp
52. Right Foot Steps Back Facing East, Step Forward To Left Front Stance, Left High Block
53. Right Hand 45 Degree Angle Cut
54. Right Hand Horizontal Cut Across Solar Plexus
55. Step Forward To Right Front Stance, Right High Block
56. Left Hand 45 Degree Angle Cut
57. Left Hand Horizontal Cut Across Solar Plexus
58. #3 Front Kick, Foot Lands In Front, Back Foot Drags To Right Cross Stance,
59. Twin High Stab
60. Left Foot Steps Back, Twin Low Block In Right Rear Stance
61. Left Foot Steps Past Right, Right Front Kick Landing Behind
62. Spin Hook Kick
63. #2 Inner Crescent Kick
64. Right Butterfly Kick
65. Left Foot Crosses Behind In X Stance Facing West. Twin Low Stab
66. Low X Block (Stabbing Behind)
67. Lift Upward High Section, Turn 180 Degrees To Left, Facing East
68. Reverse Figure 8, Twin High Stab In Left Front Stance - **Kihap**
69. Right Foot Moves To Parallel Stance, Left Foot Moves South In Long Cross Stance, Right Low Stab
70. Turn Left 180 Degrees, Left High Block
71. Right Hand Short High / Low Cut
72. Twin High Stab, Landing In Left Front Stance With A Stomp
73. Double Step Back With Right Foot Back In Long Cross Stance, Left Low Stab

Master Club Curriculum - SN

Ssahng Nat Form
"Double Kama" - Part 4 of 4

74. Turn Right 180 Degrees, Right High Block
75. Left Hand Short High / Low Cut
76. Twin High Stab, Landing In Right Front Stance With A Stomp
77. Right Foot Pulls Back To 1 Leg Stance, High / Low Block. (Left Hand High, Right Hand Low)
78. Keeping Left Hand In High Block, Right Side Kick, Landing By Turning 180 To Left. Left Foot Steps Back To One-knee Position (Left Knee Down, Facing East). Right Hand 45 Degree Angle Cut
79. Right Hand Continues With Horizontal Cut
80. Still In Kneeling Position, High Twin Stab
81. Twirl With Figure 8 Finger Roll, Reverse Grip (Both Hands Invert)
82. Stand Up, Right Foot Begins Left 360 Degree Turn To Left Back Stance
83. Right Hand Reverse Grip Figure 8 Cut
84. Right Hand Continues Figure 8 Finger Roll, Reverse Back To Straight Grip While Right Foot Moves To Back Stance
85. Left Hand Figure 8 Reverse Finger Roll To Straight Grip...
86. Continue To High / Low Block In 1 Leg Stance (Left Leg Up, Right Hand In Inner Forearm Position, Blade In).
87. Left Side Kick to Northeast, Land In Parallel Stance Facing West. Right Foot Turns 180 Degrees To Right, Landing In Right Front Stance Facing North
88. Eyes To Northeast, Cross Arms In Front, Left Hand On Top. Pull Arms Apart, Left Blade Downward Pointing Out, Right To Inner Forearm Block Position Blade In.
89. Shift To Left Front Stance Facing Northeast. Strike Crossing Arms In Front, Both Blades Pointing In (Finish Technique With Both Blades Pointing Out).
90. Twin Horizontal Stab
91. Twin Twirl Down
92. Four Way Cut - **Kihap**

June Bee: Right Foot Returns To June Bee (One Ssahng Nat in each hand crossing).
Charyut: Right Foot Steps In, Both Ssahng Nat Go To Right Hand And Bow.

Rev 4.0 - © KarateBuilt L.L.C.

My Notes on My Road to Master

Master Club
3° Black Belt Curriculum

3° Black Belt to 4° Black Belt Rank Requirements:

Congratulations again! You are now a 3° Black belt and on your way to 4°! You have already learned how important it is to persevere toward your goals. This is the time to plan your next step pn your road to Mastery... Fill out the plan on the next page and don't worry of you don't know the exact graduation months, you may look at the ProTech rotation planner to find out the months you will be graduating and what material you wil cover. This is a very exciting time - you will be working on leadership, advanced weapons and expert martial arts skills!

My Road to Mastery!

4° Black Belt Planner:

Take a minute and plan your road to 4° black belt. Your instructor can help you find the correct testing dates. At 3°, you will test every 4 months.

Current Rank	Testing For:	Requirements:	Graduation Fee:*	My Test Date
2°D	3°D	27 Classes (4 Months, 28 Months at Rank) Jung Yul, Board Breaks at Graduation, Sparring, All 2° ProTech Requirements	$80	__/__/__
3°D	Midterm#1	27 Classes (4 Months, 4 Months at Rank) Chung San, Board Breaks, Sparring, Current 3° ProTech Requirements	$80	__/__/__
3°D	Midterm#2	27 Classes (4 Months, 8 Months at Rank) Chung San, Board Breaks, Sparring, Current 3° ProTech Requirements	$80	__/__/__
3°D	Midterm#3	27 Classes (4 Months, 12 Months at Rank) Chung San, Board Breaks, Sparring, Current 3° ProTech Requirements	$80	__/__/__
3°D	Midterm#4	27 Classes (4 Months, 16 Months at Rank) Chung San, Board Breaks, Sparring, Current 3° ProTech Requirements	$80	__/__/__
3°D	Midterm#5	27 Classes (4 Months, 20 Months at Rank) Chung San, Board Breaks, Sparring, Current 3° ProTech Requirements	$80	__/__/__
3°D	Midterm#6	27 Classes (4 Months, 24 Months at Rank) Chung San, Board Breaks, Sparring, Current 3° ProTech Requirements	$80	__/__/__
3°D	Midterm#7	27 Classes (4 Months, 28 Months at Rank) Chung San, Board Breaks, Sparring, Current 3° ProTech Requirements	$80	__/__/__
3°D	Midterm#8	27 Classes (4 Months, 32 Months at Rank) Chung San, Board Breaks, Sparring, Current 3° ProTech Requirements	$80	__/__/__
3°D	4°D	27 Classes (4 Months, 36 Months at Rank) Chung San, Board Breaks at Graduation, Sparring, Special Pre-Test Training Also Required with Senior Chief Instructor	$80	__/__/__

Fourth degree black belts must also:
   be a Certified Instructor
   be 18 years old
     Application Accepted (send in 6 months prior)
Testing Must be Done at a National Event

*Graduation fees and requirements subject to change.

Rev 4.0 - © KarateBuilt L.L.C.

Master Club 3° Black Belt
ProTech Material Rotation

	March Graduation	July Graduation	November Graduation
Even Years	Mid Range Jahng Bong	Sahm Dan Bong	Oh Sung Do
Odd Years	Long Range Jahng Bong	Jee Pahng Ee	Gumdo

Required Equipment *

Korean Name	Common Name	Abbreviation	Required
Jahng Bong	Staff or Bo	JB	Yes
Jee Pahng Ee	Cane	JPE	Yes
Sahm Dan Bong	3 Sectional	SDB	Yes
Oh Sung Do	Broadsword	OSD	Yes
Gumdo	Sword	Gumdo	Yes

* For your safety, all equipment must be American Taekwondo Association / ProTech approved
** Creative Form if required must be approved by instructor

Master Club Curriculum - Forms

Name: _____

Graduation Date: __/__/__

Chung San
"Peace of Mind and Tranquility"

Your form is on the following pages. These are reprinted by permission of the American Taekwondo Association

The pattern of the form is as follows:

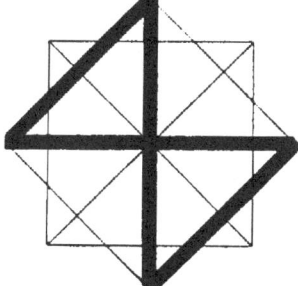

Master Club Curriculum - Forms

Chung San (Part 1)

			STANCE	SECTION
1.	R	Circular Upset Knifehand Block	P	H
2.	L	Longfist Strike	P	H
3.	L	Front Kick	--	H
4.	L	Knifehand Strike	OL	M
5.	L	Side Kick	--	M/H
6.	L	Slow Side Kick	--	M/H
7.	L	Circular Upset Knifehand Block	P	H
8.	R	Longfist Strike	P	H
9.	R	Front Kick	--	H
10.	R	Knifehand Strike	OL	M
11.	R	Side Kick	--	M/H
12.	R	Slow Side Kick	--	M/H
13.	B	Twin Vertical Palmheel Strike	F	M
14.	L	Advanced Double Knifehand Block	B	H
15.	L	#1 Round Kick	--	M
16.	L	Repeat Round Kick	--	H
17.	L	Circular Double Ridgehand Low Block	B	L
18.	L	Circular Double Knifehand Block	B	H
19.	R	Advanced Double Outer Forearm Block	B	H
20.	L	Reverse Punch	B	M
21.	R	Punch	B	M
22.	R	Circular Inner Forearm Block	B	H
23.	R	Adv Double Ridgehand Block - Ki-hap	R	H
24.	R	Slow Two Finger Strike	R	H
25.	R	Downward Palm Block	OL	L
26.	L	Jump Inner Crescent Kick	--	H
27.	L	Butterfly Kick	--	H
28.	B	Twin Elbow Strike	M	M
29.	R	Slow 9 Block (R-Knifehand, L-Fist)	F/R	L
30.	R	Front Kick	--	H
31.	R	Circular Ridgehand Block	F	H
32.	L	Reverse Two Finger Strike	F	H
33.	R	#3 Jump Front Kick	--	H
34.	B	Inner Forearm High/Low Block	P	H&L
35.	B	Ridgehand High/Low Block	P	H&L
36.	R	Outer Crescent Kick	--	H
37.	R	Spin Outer Crescent Kick	--	H
38.	B	Twin Knifehand Block	B	H

REV 4.0 - © KarateBuilt L.L.C.

Chung San (Part 2)

			STANCE	SECTION
39.	L	Upset Spearhand Strike	X	H
40.	R	Hammer Fist	B	L
41.	R	Reinforced Back Elbow Strike	B	M
42.	L	Reverse Hook Kick	--	H
43.	L	Round Kick (Continuous) - Ki-hap	--	H
44.	L	Side Kick (Continuous)	--	H
45.	L	Circular Dbl Downward Hammerfist Strike	S	H
46.	L	Downward Outer Forearm Block	R	L
47.	L	Low Openhand Sweeping Block	C	L
48.	L	Backfist Strike	S	H
49.	L	Slow 9 Block (L-Knifehand, R-Fist)	F/R	L
50.	L	Front Kick	--	H
51.	L	Circular Ridgehand Block	F	H
52.	R	Reverse Two Finger Strike	F	H
53.	L	#3 Jump Front Kick	--	H
54.	B	Inner Forearm High/Low Block	P	H&L
55.	B	Ridgehand High/Low Block	P	H&L
56.	L	Outer Crescent Kick	--	H
57.	L	Spin Outer Crescent Kick	--	H
58.	B	Twin Knifehand Block	B	H
59.	R	Upset Spearhand Strike	X	H
60.	L	Hammer Fist	B	L
61.	L	Reinforced Back Elbow Strike	B	M
62.	R	Reverse Hook Kick	--	H
63.	R	Round Kick (Continuous) - Ki-hap	--	H
64.	R	Side Kick (Continuous)	--	H
65.	R	Circular Dbl Downward Hammerfist Strike	S	H
66.	L	Slow Downward Palm Block	OL	L
67.	R	Jump Inner Crescent Kick	--	H
68.	B	Twin Hammerfist Strike	M	H
69.	R	Step Spin Heel Kick	--	H
70.	R	Jump Reverse Side Kick	--	M
71.	R	Advanced Outer Forearm Block	S	H
72.	B	Twin Vertical Palmheel Strike	F	M
73.	R	Advanced Double Knifehand Block	B	H
74.	R	#1 Round Kick	--	M
75.	R	Repeat Round Kick	--	H
76.	R	Circular Double Ridgehand Low Block	B	L

Rev 4.0 - © KarateBuilt L.L.C.

Master Club Curriculum - Forms

Chung San (Part 3)

			STANCE	SECTION
77.	R	Circular Double Knifehand Block	B	H
78.	L	Advanced Double Outer Forearm Block	B	H
79.	R	Reverse Punch	B	M
80.	L	Punch	B	M
81.	L	Circular Inner Forearm Block	B	H
82.	L	Advanced Double Ridgehand Block	R	H
83.	L	Slow Two Finger Strike	R	H

Master Club Curriculum - Breaks

Name: _____

Graduation Date: __/__/__

Board Break Requirements: 3° Black Belt

Rotation A (Even March Graduations)
Hammerfist, Upset Hammerfist (same or opposite hand), Jump Side Kick (3 obstacles)

Rotation B (Even July Graduations)
Front Kick/Side Kick (continuous kick with the same foot whithout letting it touch the floor), Spin Heel Kick with Opposite Foot (supported or speed break)

Rotation C (Even November Graduations)
Creative Board Breaks

Rotation D (Odd March Graduations)
Ridgehand, Twin Jump Front Kick, (mid or high section)

Rotation E (Odd July Graduations)
Elbow, Palm Heel, 360° Jump Reverse Side Kick

Rotation F (Odd November Graduations)
Creative Board Breaks

Board Color Guidelines
The color of board required is listed below. This is only a guide, however and students may be asked to break lighter or heavier boards based on instructor recommendation.

Age	Color	Age	Color
Under 7	White	11-12	Green
7-8	Yellow	13-15	Blue
9-10	Orange	16+ Female	Blue
		16+ Male	Brown

*Obstacle requirements are based on student size, age and rank.

Rev 4.0 - © KarateBuilt L.L.C.

 *My Notes on My Road to Master*

Master Club Curriculum - JB^{mid}

Name: _____

Graduation Date: __/__/__

Mid Range Jahng Bong Form

Your form is on the following pages. These are reprinted by permission of the American Taekwondo Association

The pattern of the form is as follows:

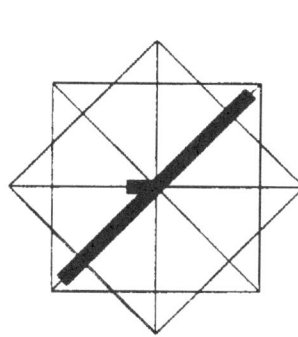

Master Club Curriculum - JB^{mid}

Mid Range Jahng Bong Form

Start Position: Stand at attention with jahng bong along right side, feet together.

Ready Position: Left foot steps to parallel stance, right hand holds jahng bong under armpit at 45 degree angle to right side.

(Kihaps are at the student's discretion)

—— **1st segment** ——

1. Bring jahng bong upward and across to left side, 180 degree spin to downward strike to low section with left leg up. (You will be on your right leg with the jahng bong pointing down with your left hand on top, palm down, and your right hand on the bottom, palm up)

2. In continuous motion, spin the jahng bong counterclockwise 360 degrees to downward strike, middle section on right side. (The jahng bong will be under your right armpit)

3. In continuous motion, rotate jahng bong upward across body to a right hand upward strike, high section, on left side.

4. Right foot steps back at a 45 degree angle to X-stance, right side downward strike to low section (jahng bong will be under right armpit).

5. Left foot slide steps back to a left rear stance, right upward strike, high section.

6. Right foot steps forward to left back stance, right upward circular strike, high section.

—— **2nd segment** ——

7. Shift to right front stance, left upward strike, low section. (Left hand is on bottom, arm extended, right hand on top)

8. Feet stay in place, rotate jahng bong to a right downward strike, high section.

9. Feet stay in place, bring left arm across for a left horizontal strike, high section. (Left arm straight, right hand holding back of jahng bong so that it touches outside of shoulder)

10. Step up to parallel stance, right downward strike, high section (back of jahng bong is under armpit).

11. Step up into a left back stance, right side strike, high section.

Rev 4.0 - © KarateBuilt L.L.C.

Mid Range Jahng Bong Form (Part 2)

12. Shift to a long right front stance, left thrust, high section.

13. Step back to a left rear stance, left circular block, high section.

—— 3rd segment ——

14. Step to a right sparring stance, weight on front, right circular downward strike, low section (on your right side).

15. Step to a left sparring stance, weight on front, right circular downward strike, low section (on your left side).

16. Step to a right sparring stance, weight on front, right circular downward strike, low section (on your right side).

17. Sweep jahng bong across to left side, spin vertical 360 on left side.

18. Sweep back to right side, spin vertical 360 to a middle block while switching to one leg stance on left leg (left hand on top, right hand low).

19. In continuous motion, set right foot down to left back stance, right downward strike, high section.

20. Shift right leg to a long front stance, right thrust to high section (right hand leading, jahng bong on left side of body).

21. Step again to long right front stance, right lunge thrust, to high section (jahng bong on left side of body).

22. Step back to a left back stance, left circular block.

—— 4th segment ——

23. Turn to back side, X-stance, right downward strike, low section.

24. Right foot steps back to right back stance, left downward strike, low section.

25. Left foot steps back to X-stance, right downward strike, low section.

26. In place, left downward strike.

27. In place, right side strike, middle section.

28. In place, left side strike, high section.

Master Club Curriculum - JB^{mid}

Mid Range
Jahng Bong Form (Part 3)

29. In place, pull down.

30. In place, right downward strike.

31. In place, left downward strike.

32. In place, raise jahng bong up, (right arm straight on top).

33. In place, downward stab.

34. Using jahng bong for pivot point, jump spin around jahng bong 180 degrees to middle stance [left hand low (palm down), right hand high (palm up)].

35. With left foot against edge of jahng bong, pop jahng bong up to horizontal position (right hand palm out, left hand palm in).

—— 5th segment ——

36. Right foot steps back to left in closed stance, middle block (jahng bong on right side, left hand on top, palm out, near back of head, right hand on the bottom, palm out).

37. Right foot steps out to middle stance, high block at 45 degrees with left hand on top and right hand on bottom, both palms facing out.

38. Step forward to a right front stance, spin jahng bong 360 degrees to a right side strike, middle section (jahng bong is under right armpit and behind back).

39. Double step to a right front stance and spin the jahng bong overhead 360 degrees counterclockwise to execute a left circular downward strike (strike goes from right upper to left middle).

—— 6th segment ——

40. Right foot steps to left foot to closed stance to face around 180 degrees. Right hand moves to front of left hand.

41. Turn 180 degrees to left front stance, with thrust to middle section.

42. In continuous motion, left foot steps to right rear stance, right downward strike, low section.

43. Step to left sparring stance, reverse figure 8 motion to X-stance with jahng bong held horizontally under chin.

Master Club Curriculum - JB^{mid}

Mid Range
Jahng Bong Form (Part 4)

44. Right foot steps to middle stance, right thrust, middle section.

45. Right foot steps across left foot to X-stance, right thrust, middle section.

46. Press down left tip of jahng bong to ground on left side, right end up.

47. Left foot steps over jahng bong, right foot steps on bottom of jahng bong (right hand high, left hand low).

48. Switch hands to left hand high, right hand low.

49. Right foot steps back, low hand pulling jahng bong up while switching to closed stance.

50. In place, bring the jahng bong horizontal under chin, right hand palm out, left arm extended.

—— 7th segment ——

Switch to baseball grip for helicopter strike

51. Right foot steps forward 90 degrees, 360 degree helicopter downward strike to low section.

52. Turn 180 degrees, 360 degree helicopter strike to low section.

53. Step back to right back stance, left hand side strike to middle section.

54. Spin jahng bong 360 degrees with left hand.

55. Right foot steps forward to left back stance, right hand side strike to high section.

—— 8th segment ——

56. Right foot steps back to right back stance, left hand downward strike, middle section.

57. Right foot steps forward, right hand figure 8.

58. Double step forward, right hand figure 8.

59. Double step forward, right hand figure 8.

60. Double step forward, right hand figure 8.

61. Double step forward, right hand figure 8.

Mid Range Jahng Bong Form (Part 5)

62. Right foot steps back, turn clockwise 180 degrees, upward strike.

—— 9th segment ——

63. Double step forward, right hand figure 8.

64. Double step forward, right hand figure 8.

65. Double step forward, right hand figure 8.

66. Double step back, right hand figure 8.

67. Double step back, right hand figure 8.

End with jahng bong under right armpit (tip low)

—— 10th segment ——

68. Right foot steps back, grip high end of jahng bong with left hand, right hand grips below left, stretch to low extended back stance (toes pointed up on left foot). Slam jahng bong flat on the ground.

69. Stand up, switch to left hand grip, then switch right hand grip, right front stance, right thrust.

70. On command, left foot steps to closed stance, go back to start position (jahng bong along right side, left hand high).

71. Spin jahng bong downward to attention stance, bow.

Jee Pahng Ee Basics

Jee Pahng Ee material is listed on the following pages. These are reprinted by permission of the American Taekwondo Association

Master Club Curriculum - JPE Basics

Jee Pahng Ee Drills

Drill #1
Left foot steps back; right backhand strike three times - high, middle, low.

Drill #2
Left foot steps back; block with wrist in (pointing gun grip); block with wrist out; thrust to eye; right backhand strike.

Drill #3
Left foot steps back; block on right side (along forearm); block to left side; right backhand swing.

Drill #4
A) Left foot steps back; figure 8 to under arm catch; bring across body to Chi-Chi position; right backhand strike.
B) Left foot steps back; figure 8 to under arm catch; two backward thrusts; left backhand strike; right backhand strike.

Drill #5
Left foot steps back; figure 8 to catch; over shoulder to left hand and number one line strike with back of hook; switch to right hand and right backhand strike.

Drill #6
Step back with right foot and throw Jee Pahng Ee up and catch with right hand 2/3 of the way down shaft; number one and number two line strike with back of hook; pass to left hand spinning five times; grab with right hand and backhand strike.

Drill #7
Fish hook; step back with left foot and hook hand, weapon or neck; butt strike to face; drop to one knee and butt strike to shin; spear foot with tip and stand up; right backhand strike.

Drill #8
Put right hand through hook, grab shaft with left hand; rotate wrist twice, blocking with second; thrust tip to midsection; hook down, strike to groin; number two line strike with tip.

Drill #9
Throw Jee Pahng Ee up with right hand while stepping back with right foot and catch shaft with right hand. helicopter, two hits (head then leg); right backhand strike spinning 360° on right foot; left backhand strike; switch to right hand and right backhand strike.

Name: _____

Graduation Date: __/__/__

Jee Pahng Ee (Cane) Form

Your form is on the following pages. These are reprinted by permission of the American Taekwondo Association

The pattern of the form is as follows:

Master Club Curriculum - JPE

Jee Pahng Ee Form (Part 1)

Start: Begin by facing east.
Attention: Feet together, with cane in right hand (as in walking position). Bow.
June Bee: Step to the left with left foot, feet shoulder width apart. Move hook of cane to the centerline of your body (leave point of cane on same ground position), and place left hand over right.

1. Step left foot to right foot (heels touching, "L" position), step right foot to North, right sparring stance, right hand, #8 line position

2. Step left foot to right foot, right foot steps clockwise to South, right foot steps to right sparring stance, right hand, #8 line position

3. No step, right hand, figure 8

4. No step, right hand, figure 8, to under arm position

5. Step left foot to right foot, grip cane with left hand, turn to North, #9 thrust (2 hands), right front stance

6. Step right foot counterclockwise 180, then left foot 180 counterclockwise (jumping), circle swing (end position in left armpit)

7. Spin 360 clockwise on right foot

8. Grip cane with left hand, #3 side kick to knee (no re-chamber), land in middle stance, 270 horizontal swing (left to right), pull cane back to left hand

9. Step left foot forward to North (while ducking), right reverse hook kick, land in right sparring stance, 270 horizontal swing

10. Step left foot to right, closed stance, 2 full circle swings counterclockwise. Turn North-East, step right foot to right sparring stance, point cane point to opponents face, block with hook of cane to left (leaving cane point in place)

11. Block with hook of cane to right (leaving cane point in place)

12. Step right foot forward further, leaning weight forward, thrust point of cane into face

13. Pull right foot back (shortening the stance), #8 downward strike

REV 4.0 - © KarateBuilt L.L.C.

Jee Pahng Ee Form (Part 2)

14. In place, stab cane point into opponent's foot

15. Shuffle step back to North-East, lift cane up, blocking to right side

16. Chamber cane to left side, using left hand for extra support, strike to the groin

17. Right foot slides forward, pivoting 180 counterclockwise, facing North-West, step left foot to North-East into middle stance, thread cane behind opponent's front knee and in front of back knee

18. Right foot step clockwise to North-East, motion with cane causes legs to buckle and opponent to fall

19. Double step left to right, right to sparring stance, hook opponent's right arm

20. Thrust hook to opponent's face

21. Hook opponent's left arm

22. Thrust hook to opponent's face

23. Strike groin with cane point

24. Hook neck from right side, use left hand on right wrist for extra support

25. Pull head down with cane and right hand

26. Left knee to midsection

27. Step left foot to West pulling opponent down with hook of cane behind the neck (kneeling)

28. Facing East, cross-step right foot back past left foot and left foot back, strike opponent's head with cane point, face

29. Toss up cane, switching ends, strike opponent with hook end

30. Toss up cane, spinning in the air 3 or 4 times, catch with left hand

31. Right foot steps back to left sparring stance, pass cane behind back, grab with right hand (jahng bong twirling position)

32. Left foot steps back to right sparring stance, spin cane in right hand, pass cane behind back, grab with left hand (jahng bong twirling position)

Jee Pahng Ee Form (Part 3)

33. Right foot steps back to left sparring stance, triangle strike

34. Left foot steps back to right sparring stance, pass cane behind back to right hand, triangle strike

35. Right hand, #1 line strike, end with cane under left armpit, left hand on right forearm (ankle lock position)

36. Step right foot back to x-stance, thrust cane hook to shin

37. Pivot to West, fan strike

38. Step right foot to West into middle stance, holding cane with right hand and laying in palm of left hand

39. Support spin cane one time (clockwise), pull cane down to right side

40. Pull cane up to front of body (horizontal to floor), grab with both hands

41. Jump up, right front kick to West, same time, "mule kick" to East (to opponent's groin), land in middle stance

42. Press block downward, hook of cane in left hand, right hand farther down cane

43. Turn South-West, step left foot to left sparring stance, point cane point to opponents face, block with hook of cane to right (leaving cane point in place)

44. Block with hook of cane to left (leaving cane point in place)

45. Step left foot forward further, leaning weight forward, thrust point of cane into face

46. Pull left back (shortening the stance), #8 downward strike

47. In place, stab cane point into opponent's foot

48. Shuffle step back to South-West, lift cane up, blocking to right side

49. Chamber cane to right side, using right hand for extra support, strike to the groin

50. Left foot slides forward, pivoting 180 clockwise, facing South-East, step right foot to South-West into middle stance, thread cane behind opponent's front knee and in front of back knee

Jee Pahng Ee Form (Part 4)

51. Left foot step clockwise to South-West, motion with cane causes legs to buckle and opponent to fall

52. Double step right to left, left to sparring stance, hook opponent's left arm

53. Thrust hook to opponent's face

54. Hook opponent's right arm

55. Thrust hook to opponent's face

56. Strike groin with cane point

57. Hook neck from left side

58. Pull head down with cane and left hand

59. Right knee to midsection

60. Swing cane clockwise

61. Double step right foot to left, left foot to left sparring stance facing East, point cane to opponent's face

62. In place, left hand, #8 line position

63. Step right foot to left foot, right foot steps counterclockwise to West, left foot steps to left sparring stance, left hand, #8 line position

64. No step, left hand, figure 8

65. No step, left hand, figure 8, to under arm position

66. Step right foot to left foot, grip cane with right hand, turn to East, #9 thrust (2 hands), left front stance

67. Step left foot clockwise 180, then right foot 180 clockwise (jumping), circle swing (end position in right armpit)

68. Spin 360 counterclockwise on left foot

69. Grip cane with right hand, #3 side kick to knee (no re-chamber), land in middle stance, 270 horizontal swing (right to left), pull cane back to right hand

Jee Pahng Ee Form (Part 5)

70. Step right foot forward to East (while ducking), left reverse hook kick, land in left sparring stance, 270 horizontal swing

71. Step right foot to left, closed stance, 2 full circle swings clockwise

Left foot returns to ready position

Left foot returns to attention

Long Range Jahng Bong Floor Drills

Long Range Jahng Bong material is listed on the following pages. These are reprinted by permission of the American Taekwondo Association

Long Range Jahng Bong Floor Drills

Drill #1 - Double Top Grip, Front Stance
  Switch Hand Strike

Drill #1b - Over / Under Grip, Front Stance
  Switch Hand Strike

Drill #2 - Over / Under Grip, Cross Stance, Front Stance
  Low Tip Block and Strike

Drill #3 - Double Top Grip, Middle Stance
  Middle Strike

Drill #4 - Double Top Grip, Front Stance
  Low Block

Drill #5 - Double Top Grip, Front Stance
  Low Block and High Strike

Drill #6 - Double Top Grip, Front Stance
  Low Block and Side Strike.

Drill #7 - Single Hand Grip, Long Front Stance
  Low Block, One Hand Long Strike

Drill #8 - Over / Under Grip, Cross Stance
  Cross Strike, Pan, Pick Up.

Drill #9 - Over / Under Grip, Cross Stance, Front Stance
  Stab

Long Range Jahng Bong Form

Your form is on the following pages. These are reprinted by permission of the American Taekwondo Association

The pattern of the form is as follows:

Master Club Curriculum - JB^{long}

Long Range
Jahng Bong Form - Part 1

Attention Jahng Bong on Right Side

1. Left hand across to grab Jahng Bong
   Pull stick up with left hand and pull to high low downward circle block leaving right hand at tip of stick.
   (Jahng Bong is at a 45 Degree Angle across your body)

2. 45 Degree step with left foot
   Long Jahng Bong strike high

3. Slide left hand to tip
   step right foot long upward strike
   switch Right palm

4. Right hand pass tip behind strike

5. Left Downward strike (Face Front)

6. Turn Counter Clockwise - Jahng Bong turn Clock Wise over head
   180 degree strike

7. Upward strike and downward strike same time.

8. Left hand back to tip of Jahng Bong
   Shift to Combat Stance
   Long Thrust twisting palm up

9. Pull Jahng Bong back to Short Sparring Stance

10. Step Right foot long Jahng Bong Strike

11. Slide foot in and back out with Jahng Bong circle and Repeat Long Strike

Long Range Jahng Bong Form - Part 2

12. Left hand slide to right hand to tip
    Turn counter Clockwise 180 degrees Long Combat Stance
    Thrust and Pull

13. Turn Clockwise with Clearing Strike (Arm Across Body)

14. Figure 8

15. Figure 8

16. Figure 8

17. Low Squat Back Stance and Low Ground Strike

18. Stand up to Middle Stance
    Counter Clockwise Hook Block with Short Stab

19. Step Back with Right Foot Long downward
    Strike Left Hand forward

20. Long Downward Strike Right Hand Forward

21. Long Upward Strike

22. Long Thrust and Pull

23. Shift to X Stance Long Jahng Bong Strike Right Hand Forward

24. Figure 8 with Horizontal Block, Side Strike coming from over your head

25. Left floor step Half Figure 8 Strike with Left Hand up

26. Left Hand slide to tip (right hand palm up) Combat Stance

Long Range
Jahng Bong Form - Part 3

27. Long Jahng Bong Strike Low

28. Long Stance to Cross Stance (pick up)

29. Circle Sweep Right Foot Stomp Long Downward Strike - land in a Middle Stance

30. Right Foot shift back to Closed Stance

31. Figure 8

   (Step with each figure 8 end with left foot forward)

32. Figure 8

33. Figure 8

34. Figure 8

35. Figure 8

36. Figure 8

37. Long Over Head Tip Strike in a Front Stance

38. Jahng Bong release

39. Right Shoulder Body Roll

40. Grab Right hand 1 (One) Arm Circle Sweep over head

41. 1 (One) Arm Circle Sweep to behind back

42. Grab with Left hand rolling across belly Clockwise switching to right hand

Long Range
Jahng Bong Form - Part 4

43. Right hand up over head V-Roll

44. Palm to Palm roll behind the back

45. V - Roll up to Middle Stance left hand finishing. Jahng Bong point to Left Side

46. 360 Degree Belly Roll with Body turning Clockwise.

47. Back Counter Clock wise with 360 degree Belly Roll

48. From Middle to Sparring Stance.
    Right hand under with upward strike to chin

49. Down Strike to Collar Bone

50. Clockwise Strike to Head and
    Downward Strike to Collar Bone

51. Left hand Rotate to top of Jahng Bong

52. Figure 8 (Back to Starting point, between 3-6 count Figure 8)

53. Figure 8

54. Figure 8

55. Finish Right side with pressing Knife Hand Block

56. Left hand cross under Jahng Bong , spin Clockwise to left side then to right side.

# My Notes on My Road to Master

Sahm Dahm Bong Drills

Sahm Dahm Bong material is listed on the following pages. These are reprinted by permission of the American Taekwondo Association

Master Club Curriculum - SDB Basics

Sahm Dahm Bong Drills

1. Three Count - right, left & right straight down.

2. Three Count - right, left & right fan.

3. Three Count - right, left & right dips down and comes up for downward strike.

4. Golf Swing - right, left, right, right blocks low and left comes high and circles to a one leg stance, high standing staff block.

5. X Block (right on top) - right downward strike, right fan, right downward strike (short), right throwing strike (middle), pull around and throwing strike (long).

6. Strike Stick - left thrust to side, right thrust to front.

7. Strike Stick - left throwing strike swing around back and catch, left & right side strike at the same time, twin downward thrust to floor, twin downward strike.

8. Strike Stick - throw up right hand and catch middle section, right figure eight followed by three forward rolls to foot stop, flip up and catch in right hand back to "U" position.

9. Strike Stick - right downward throwing strike, pick up with foot flip and catch on right side, middle "U" block, followed by second middle "U" block, swing around head and step over, swing around head again and safety roll, swing along floor and catch behind back, left strike to side, right strike to front (kihap).

*** Start all nine drills with your right foot forward ***

Sahm Dahm Bong Form

The Sahm Dahm Bong form is on the following pages. These are reprinted by permission of the American Taekwondo Association

Sahm Dahm Bong Form

Start: Begin by facing east.
Attention: Feet together, with weapon folded in right arm.
June Bee: With the right hand holding on to one end, grab the other end with the left hand so both ends are sticking up, then tap ends twice and bow.

1. Right foot steps east to a left backstance, right hand #1 angle strike

2. (no step) Left hand #1 angle strike

3. (no step) Right hand #8 angle strike / left hand under arm

4. Pivot right foot left foot steps west to front stance (right hand swing over head) right hand #5 angle strike

5. Left foot pivots, right foot steps south to a front stance and execute a right hand low strike

6. (no step) Left hand low strike

7. (no step) Right hand high fan strike (clockwise)

8. Step right foot to left foot, then left foot steps west to a front stance and right hand low strike

9. Pivot on left foot, then step east with the right foot to a rear stance and right hand high strike

10. (no step) Left hand high strike

11. (no step) Right hand poke (while lifting up right foot)

12. Step down right foot, left foot steps to X-stance, execute a cross hit

13. Spin counter clockwise 180 degrees extend weapon out to sides with both arms

14. Step left foot east to front stance, right hand low strike

15. (no step) Left hand low strike while at the same time right hand executes a high fan

16. Step left foot to right foot face south, low X-block

17. (no step) Cross hit

Sahm Dahm Bong Form - Pt. 2

18. Left hand big circle low block into left 1 legged stance

19. Step right foot to south then left foot to south

20. Jump into X-stance executing an X-block

21. (no step) Right hand high strike to south

22. (no step) Right hand high fan strike to south

23. Hold weapon in left hand while right hand throws other end of weapon to the ground

24. Right hand grips weapon next to left hand, left hand releases

25. Right hand swings weapon over to the ground

26. Lift right hand so weapon comes up and grab weapon with the left hand

27. Stepping with the right foot, turn 360 degrees to right back stance facing south

28. Toss weapon up with right hand to switch grip

29. (no step) Left hand high strike

30. Right foot steps forward and right hand executes a high strike

31. Left foot steps behind right foot to left back stance facing north while executing right hand high strike

32. (no step) Right hand low strike

33. Left foot steps forward and execute a left low circle block while raising right foot ending up in a left one legged stance

34. Right foot steps down to left back stance

35. Hold weapon in left hand while right hand throws other end of weapon to the ground

36. Right hand grips weapon next to left hand, left hand releases

37. Right hand raises weapon up, right foot kicks end of weapon landing in a right back stance while grabbing weapon with left hand and execute C-block (right hand high)

38. Right foot steps forward, then left foot (spin) steps forward ending in a right back stance while executing right hand helicopter and C-block (left hand high)

Sahm Dahm Bong Form - Pt. 3

39. (no step) Rotate weapon to right side C-block (right hand high)
40. Release weapon with left hand and lasso over head
41. Lasso low stepping over weapon first with the left foot and then with the right
42. Lasso over head once stepping forward and spin lasso again
43. Safety low
44. Crouch down with right foot in front and weapon behind the back (ends of weapon are pointing front) facing north
45. (no step) Left thrust to west
46. (no step) Right thrust to north
47. Stand up into closed stance (facing west) low X-block
48. Strike out to both sides (striking to north and south)
49. Right foot steps to south (facing east) weapon behind back (ends of weapon are pointing front)
50. Weapon comes over head stab ends into ground
51. Cross ends of weapon lifting up to strike out to both sides (striking to north and south)
52. (no step) Right hand X-pattern
53. (no step) Right hand low strike
54. (no step) Right hand tosses up weapon, grab middle section with right hand
55. (no step) Figure 8
56. Step back twirl weapon three times
57. Step forward figure 8
58. Step back twirl weapon three times
59. Stop twirl with right foot

Sahm Dahm Bong Form - Pt. 4

60. Toss end of weapon up and grab with right hand

61. Right hand high strike then toss weapon behind back and catch with right hand (weapon will be behind the back with ends pointing front) facing east

62. Weapon comes over head stab ends into ground

63. Cross ends of weapon lifting up to strike out to both sides (striking to north and south)

64. Left foot steps north into a straight front stance and right hand thrust

65. Turn counter clockwise into a right straight front stance and left hand thrust

66. Pivot to face east and right hand thrust

67. (no step) Left low strike and right high fan

Step right foot to left and fold weapon into right arm

My Notes on My Road to Master

Oh Sung Do (OSD) Form

The Oh Sung Do form is on the following pages. These are reprinted by permission of the American Taekwondo Association

Oh Sung Do Form

Name: _____
Graduation Date: __/__/__

Gumdo (Sword) Form

The Gumdo (Sword) form is on the following pages. These are reprinted by permission of the American Taekwondo Association

Gumdo Form

Gumdo Form

Gumdo Form

Creative Form Requirements

At 3° degree black belt, you are learning to become a high rank in Taekwondo. When you become a Master, your form will have moves that you develop in addition to the standard form. As a 3° Degree, you may develop a "form" that will be demonstrated at a Graduation as part of your midterm.

The requirements are:
1) It must be written and submitted to your instructor prior to graduation.
2) Approval must be granted by instructor.
3) It may include ONLY weapons that are in our regular system.
4) You must turn in the following 2 pages.
5) Maximum length of form is 1 minute.

Master Club Curriculum - Creative Form

My 3° Creative Form:

Include all weapons, props, people required, or materials. It should be a complete description.

My 3° Creative Form: Announcement

This is for the MC at the Graduation to read to describe your creative form to the audience. Please include all philosophy and physical explanation. Also include when they should speak or any other instructions (ex: "When the music starts, say this_____")

Master Club Curriculum - Application

Application to Test for 4° Black Belt:

You must send the application into National Headquarters 6 months prior to testing for 4° Black Belt. You must also be 18 to test. This application is included for reference and is subject to change - you must send in the most up-to-date version (verify with your instructor).

To: All 3rd Degree Black Belts   Updated 7/19/2011

Re: MIDTERM & TESTING APPLICATION and CHECKLIST

As of November 2003 an individual wanting to test <u>from</u> 3rd Degree to 4th Degree Black Belt may test at a <u>National</u> Tournament as well as World Championships.

> **Midterm**: Page -2- of the following application should be sent to ATA Headquarters <u>30 days</u> in advance of the event you wish to midterm at.

1. **Rank Test:** Complete the <u>entire application</u> following this checklist. It must be received at ATA Headquarters <u>6 months</u> in advance of the event you wish to <u>Test</u> at (**no exceptions**).
2. Approval / denial letters will be sent out no later than 30 days prior to the date of the event.
3. All other requirements must be completed and received (if appropriate) at headquarters no later thank 30 days in advance of the event date, or an individual will be dropped from the midterm / testing roster (no excuses accepted). Special Note: See "Testing Rules" for Fit Test requirements.
4. If a no change is received at rank testing, applicant may retest in-region with their instructor's permission, however there must be at least <u>two judges</u> on the testing panel that are the rank of 6th degree or higher! Re-test may also be done at Fall or Spring Nationals or a World Championship event.

Midterm Requirements:
- Payment in full enclosed with application: Midterm Fee is $100 per midterm
- Age Requirement minimum – 16 years old
- Senior Instructor must approve & sign application (**will be denied if not approved/signed!**)

Rank Test requirements
- Senior Instructor must approve & sign application (**will be denied of not approved/signed!**)
- ATA Fit Test passed (required for World's & Nationals 3rd degree test applicants starting at World's 2009)
- Payment in full enclosed with application
   Test fee is $300 – less mid-term fees paid (3 mid-terms at $100 each)
- Time in Rank - <u>3 years</u> from the date of receiving 3rd Degree to the date of testing
- Age Requirement – 18 years old
- Mid-Terms must be complete (and in house at HQ no later than 30 days prior to the event)
- Instructor Status – must be **one** of the following (no later than 30 days prior to the event)
   __ Level 1Trainer (certification level 1 completed) minimum required to test
   __ Specialty Trainer (certification level 2 completed)
   __ Certified Instructor
- Certification must be current (no later than 30 days prior to the event!)
- Regional and National Participation (will be verified via regional seniors)
- School Owners   __Testing results sent to HQ Pd in full and up-to-date
                       __ ATA account must be paid in full
                       __ WMA account must be paid in full

TESTING / MIDTERM APPLICATION

Use this application if you are **presently** a 3rd Degree Black Belt   (Updated 7/19/2011)

Midterm: Page -2- of this application should be sent to ATA Headquarters 30 days in advance of the event you wish to midterm at. Midterm applicants are subject to denial.

Rank Test: Testing for the rank of 4th Degree must be completed at a National tournament or World Championship event. Complete pages 2 - 3 of his application. Completed form must be received by the Master's Council at ATA International Headquarters **SIX MONTH** prior to the date of the event. Please note that applications may be denied; approval/denial letters will be mailed out no later than 30 days prior to the event. **Applicants will be denied if ALL REQUIREMENTS are not complete within 30 days of the event. Approval letters are mailed 30 days prior to the scheduled event.**

I wish to: Midterm ___   Rank Test ___   At (date/location): _____

Name: _____   Age ____   Birthdate ____

ATA # ____   Inst. # ____   Rank (I am) ____   Date of Rank ____

Address _____

City _____   State/Country _____   Zip _____

Email Address _____

Home Phone ( ) _____   Alternate Phone ( ) _____

My Instructor's name is _____

My School Owner's name is _____

Physical material approved by my Inst. (3 items I will perform)   *TKD Form ____   Protech ____

Sparring ____   Topic: ____   Board Breaks ____   Consisting of ____

*Substituting Protech for TKD Form at a National/World Event requires explanation and the Grand Master's approval

Amount enclosed $ _____

I authorize investigation of all statements contained in this application. I understand that misrepresentation or omission of facts called for is cause for rejection of application. I understand that if I do not get my seniors approval and permission to test or midterm, I shall be denied by ATA HQ. I understand that I must have my senior's signature of approval **PRIOR** to applying to ATA HQ.   Senior's Signature denotes approval. Do not sign if not approved.

_____   _____   _____   _____
Applicant's Signature   Date   Senior Instructor's Signature   Date

ATA Fit Test: Date Completed _____   Pass: Yes ____   No ____

Required for World's & Nationals 3rd Degree test applicants starting at World Championships 2009 and after!
ATA Fit Test is good for 12 months from date of "passing".
ATA Fit Tests are available at Fall / Spring / BB Nationals and World Championships.
Register on line during regular tournament registration or call the Instruction Dept at 1-501-568-2821

Leadership Points are required for rank test applicants who ARE 4th degree or higher: Due to the fact that this requirement became mandatory, with NO grandfather clause, prior to detailed record keeping, each applicant must compare their personal records to the records on his/her member file online. If something is missing attach a separate sheet to the high rank test application with the following information (or email an excel file to melanie.morris@ataonline.com):

Name of topic	Date	Location	Host	Instructor of topic

h/tsh/testing/appsasofsep08/testapp3rddegjan11.doc   (Updated 7/19/2011)

Midterms: Dates and Locations: _____ _____
_____ _____

Tournament Judge: Certification Level _____ Expire Date _____

Instructor Status: Certified ___ Specialty Certified (Lvl 2) ___ Certified Trainer (Lvl 1) ___ (min req.)
Date Certified (black collar): _____ Expire Date _____
Membership expiration date (if Level 1 Trainer or Level 2 Specialty): _____

Re-certification or member renewal **must be completed** 30 days prior to the event. Applicants will be denied if this requirement is not met!

If not a school or club owner, at whose facility do you teach or manage?
Name: _____ Location _____ School # _____
Name: _____ Location _____ School # _____

School/Club Owner: Licensed facilities you have owned (if extra space is needed, attach additional pages)
#_____ Location _____ Date: from – to _____ Avg. # testing _____
#_____ Location _____ Date: from – to _____ Avg. # testing _____
#_____ Location _____ Date: from – to _____ Avg. # testing _____
#_____ Location _____ Date: from – to _____ Avg. # testing _____

Your Junior Instructors who own schools or clubs: (if extra space is needed, attach additional pages)
Name _____ #_____ Location _____
Name _____ #_____ Location _____
Name _____ #_____ Location _____
Name _____ #_____ Location _____

FOR HQ OFFICE USE ONLY: Pd _____ Paid Via _____ Date Received _____

Date App Rcvd _____
Rank _____ Time in Rank _____   If School/Club Owner: Account Info
ATA Fit _____ Age Req _____   School _____ ATA _____ WMA _____
Inst. Status _____ Exp. _____   School _____ ATA _____ WMA _____
Midterms _____   School _____ ATA _____ WMA _____
_____
_____

Training Instructor Approval _____   Testings submitted timely: _____
Senior of Record Approval _____   Notes:

Master Club

4° Black Belt Curriculum

ATA
BLACK BELT ACADEMY

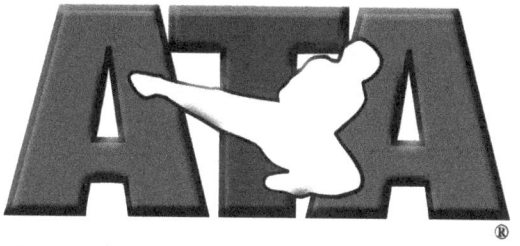

4° Black Belt to 5° Black Belt Rank Requirements:

Congratulations! As a 4° Black Belt you are now a "High Rank"! The next step is 5° and then you are within sight of becoming a "Master". Now you may start attending leadership camp and working on even more advanced material. Fill out the plan on the next page and start your next step on your road to Master.

Note: Applications and forms required by ATA are subject to change. Check with your instructor to verify you're sending in the proper forms for testing application.

My Road to Mastery!

5° Black Belt Planner:

Take a minute and plan your road to 5° black belt.
Your instructor can help you find the correct dates.
At 4°, you should plan on midterming every 12 months.

Current Rank	Testing For:	Requirements:	Graduation Fee:*	My Grad Date
3°	4°	4 Months, 36 Months at Rank Chung San, Board Breaks at Graduation, Sparring, Current 3° ProTech Requirements (at School) **Testing Must be Done at a National Event**	$80	_/_/_
4°	Midterm#1	4 Months, 4 Months at Rank Sok Bong, Board Breaks, Sparring, Current 4° ProTech Requirements	$80	_/_/_
4°	Midterm#2	4 Months, 8 Months at Rank Sok Bong, Board Breaks, Sparring, Current 4° ProTech Requirements	$80	_/_/_
4°	Midterm#3	4 Months, 12 Months at Rank Sok Bong, Board Breaks, Sparring, Current 4° ProTech Requirements	$80	_/_/_
4°	Midterm#4	4 Months, 16 Months at Rank Sok Bong, Board Breaks, Sparring, Current 4° ProTech Requirements	$80	_/_/_
4°	Midterm#5	4 Months, 20 Months at Rank Sok Bong, Board Breaks, Sparring, Current 4° ProTech Requirements	$80	_/_/_
4°	Midterm#6	4 Months, 24 Months at Rank Sok Bong, Board Breaks, Sparring, Current 4° ProTech Requirements	$80	_/_/_
4°	Midterm#7	4 Months, 28 Months at Rank Sok Bong, Board Breaks, Sparring, Current 4° ProTech Requirements	$80	_/_/_
4°	Midterm#8	4 Months, 32 Months at Rank Sok Bong, Board Breaks, Sparring, Current 4° ProTech Requirements	$80	_/_/_
4°	Midterm#9	4 Months, 36 Months at Rank Sok Bong, Board Breaks, Sparring, Current 4° ProTech Requirements	$80	_/_/_
4°	Midterm#10	4 Months, 40 Months at Rank Sok Bong, Board Breaks, Sparring, Current 4° ProTech Requirements	$80	_/_/_
4°	Midterm#11	4 Months, 44 Months at Rank Sok Bong, Board Breaks, Sparring, Current 4° ProTech Requirements	$80	_/_/_
4°	5°	4 Months, 48 Months at Rank Sok Bong, Board Breaks at Graduation, Sparring, **Current Certified Instructor,** **ATA Application Accepted (send in 6 months prior)** **Special Pre-Test Training Also Required with Senior Chief Instructor** **Testing Must be Done at World Championships**	ATA Fee	_/_/_

*Graduation fees and requirements subject to change. All graduations are at instructor discretion.

Rev 4.0 - © KarateBuilt L.L.C.

Master Club 4° Black Belt
ProTech Material Rotation

Type	Even Years			Odd Years		
	March Graduation	July Graduation	November Graduation	March Graduation	July Graduation	November Graduation
Regular	Sahm Dahm Bong	Creative	Long Range Jahng Bong	Jee Pahng Ee	Gumdo	Mid Range Jahng Bong
Supplemental	1° BME Form	1° SJB Form	2° Ssahng Nat Form	2° DSJB Form	2° DBME Form	1° Knife Form

*Supplemental material is for in-class training. While not a primary requirement for testing/midterms 4° and up students are responsible for all lower rank material.

Required Equipment – Same as 3°*

* For your safety, all equipment must be American Taekwondo Association / ProTech approved
** Creative Form if required must be approved by instructor

SOK BONG POOME-SAE
FOURTH DEGREE BLACK BELT

2/24/04 5:00 pm

Translates as "Crest of Granite Mountain"
Interpretation is "You will live comfortably and in peace"

NEW KICKS: Step jump spin heel kick. [56]
                    Sweep. [3]

NEW BLOCKS: High-low palm heel block. [34]
                    "C" block. [55,58]
                    Twin downward palm heel block. [63]
                    Double ridgehand block. [54,57,84]

NEW STRIKES: Double knifehand strike. [1,52]
                    Twin upset knifehand strike. [14]
                    Upset arc hand strike. [40]
                    Circle downward hammerfist strike. [41]
                    Twin palm heel push to sides. [67]
                    Twin back elbow strike. [66]
                    First-finger strike. [26]
                    Augmented downward hammerfist strike. [79]
                    Augmented downward backfist strike. [80]
                    (Elbow of striking arm on back fist of other arm.)

NEW PUNCHES: "C" punch. [13]
                    First-knuckle punch. [25]

NEW STANCES: Long stance. [11,44]
                    Knee stance. [5, 6, 7, 8, 9, 48, 49, 50, 51]

Form should take about 2:05 to 2:10 minutes from attention to final bow
All advanced open hand techniques begin in a closed hand position (fist)

READY STANCE: Right knifehand 1/2 command stance (right foot steps to parallel stance as arms are positioned).

☆ June Bee - Half command stance.

6

1. Right foot jumps east to right X-stance, ball of left foot should be 1 sparring stance length from center; double knifehand strike to east middle section.
2. Pivot 180 degrees counterclockwise, left spin heel kick to east high section, left foot lands (on center point) in sparring stance, facing west.
3. Right knee drops to floor, right hand drops to floor; left sweep (bottom of foot sweeps ankle level in motion like heel kick) to east. And...

WORLD TRADITIONAL TAEKWONDO UNION HEADQUARTERS
6210 Baseline Road, Little Rock, Arkansas 72209 / 501-568-4181

SOK BONG POOME-SAE
FOURTH DEGREE BLACK BELT

6
4. In a continuous motion, left round kick to southeast.
5. Left foot lands east to right knee stance (similar to back stance, but with rear knee on floor in line with front heel; instep on floor), right upset knifehand block to southeast high section.
6. No step, left vertical punch to southeast middle section.

3
7. No step, simultaneous left knifehand high block, right upset knifehand strike to east high section.
8. No step, left arc hand strike to east high section.
9. No step, right high upward elbow strike to left palm toward east.

7
10. Jump to middle stance with left foot in position, right foot stepping east, double outer forearm block to east.
11. Left foot moves west to long stance (left foot on center point) (four foot lengths wide; rear leg pivoted to rear and knee bent 90 degrees, front leg is extended), right downward palm heel block to east with tension (5 seconds) as right leg straightens.
12. Left foot steps to right, right jump side kick to east middle or high section. Land feet together facing north.
13. Pivot 180 degrees counterclockwise, left foot steps east to right back stance, C-punch (middle & high section) to east.
14. Right foot shifts to form left front stance to east, high twin upset knifehand strike to east, neck level. And...
15. In a continuous motion, twin knifehand block to east.
16. Right foot pulls to shield left knee in left one legged stance (left foot on east point), twin punch to east high section.

---(Direction Change on Line Corner)---

5
17. Left jump front kick to northeast high section; right foot lands 1 sparring stance length southwest (on diagonal); left foot does not step down.
18. No step, in place, right jump front kick to southeast high section. Left foot lands in place; right does not step down.
19. Left jump front kick to northwest high section. Right foot lands in place, then left foot lands to the southwest to form left back stance toward northeast.
20. No step, tension (5 seconds) double knifehand low block to northeast.
21. Pivot in place to right back stance, tension (5 seconds) double knifehand block to southwest.

6
22. Right foot steps together to left foot, right jump round kick to southwest. Land 1 rear stance to southwest in right sparring stance. And...
23. In a continuous motion, left spin crescent kick to southwest.
24. Land in left back stance, double outer forearm block to southwest. Kihap.
25. No step, left reverse first knuckle upset punch to southwest midsection.
26. Left foot steps to right, right steps forward to left back stance (right foot on south point), left

WORLD TRADITIONAL TAEKWONDO UNION HEADQUARTERS
6210 Baseline Road, Little Rock, Arkansas 72209 / 501-568-4181

SOK BONG POOME-SAE
FOURTH DEGREE BLACK BELT

6
    reverse first finger strike to southwest high section.
27. #2 Left inner crescent kick to southwest, (prepare to land to north).

---(Direction Change on Line Corner)---

4
28. Land in right rear stance to north (right foot at center point), left inward palm heel block to midsection.
29. No step, right reverse punch to north middle section. And...
30. In a continuous motion, no step, left punch to north middle section. And...
31. In a continuous motion, no step, right reverse punch to north high section.

3
32. Left foot steps north to right back stance, double inner forearm block to north high section.
33. No step, right high, left low block to north.
34. No step, left high, right low palm heel block (high blocks upwards, low blocks down-wards with tension (5 seconds)

7
35. #2 right front kick to north low section. And...
36. In a continuous motion, right round kick. And...
37. In a continuous motion, right hook kick.
38. Land in middle stance to north. Left foot steps to right for #3 hook kick to north. And...
39. In a continuous motion, right round kick to north.
40. Right foot lands on center point in left back stance, right upset arc hand strike to north, neck level.
41. Left foot steps to right in closed stance to north (both feet on center point), left circular downward hammerfist strike to right palm, middle section.

---(Direction Change on Line Corner)---

3
42. Right foot steps clockwise west to right back stance to east (right foot on center point), circle double downward knifehand strike to east, slow. (2 seconds)
43. #1 left side kick to east.
44. Retracting leg, turn clockwise 180 degrees to land (body faces north), in long stance (four foot lengths wide; rear leg pivoted to rear and knee bent 90 degrees, front leg is extended), tension left downward palm heel block to west as left leg straightens (5 seconds). Kihap.

7
45. Left foot shifts to left back stance to east, middle knifehand X-block to east.
46. Left foot steps together to right foot; left knee sets down to west, both palms on floor to west, right side kick to east. And...
47. In a continuous motion, repeat right side kick to east.
48. Right lands to left foot, left foot moves 1 rear stance west to right knee stance (similar to back stance, but with rear knee on floor in line with front heel; instep on floor), simultaneous left

SOK BONG POOME-SAE
FOURTH DEGREE BLACK BELT

7
- knifehand high block, right vertical ridgehand strike to west, groin level.
- 49. No step, left upset knifehand block to west high section. And...
- 50. In a continuous motion, no step, right reverse punch to west middle section. And...
- 51. In a continuous motion, left punch to west middle section.

4
- 52. Jump up 1 rear stance length to west to left X-stance, double knifehand strike to west, middle section.
- 53. Right spin heel kick to west high section.
- 54. Right foot lands to east in right back stance to west, slow (2 seconds) double ridgehand block to west high section.
- 55. No step, C-block (as if grabbing an attacker's stick, middle & high section) to west.

4
- 56. Right foot steps west 1 sparring stance length, left jump spin heel kick to west.
- 57. Land in left back stance to west (right foot on west point), double ridgehand block to west high section.
- 58. No step, slow (2 seconds) C-block (as if grabbing an attacker's stick, middle & high section) to west.
- 59. Left foot pulls to shield right knee in right one legged stance (right foot on west point), twin punch to west high section.

---(Direction Change on Line Corner)---

4
- 60. Right jump front kick to southwest, left foot lands 1 sparring stance length northeast (on diagonal), right foot does not step down.
- 61. No step, left jump front kick to southeast. Right foot lands in place, left leg does not step down.
- 62. No step, in place right jump front kick to northwest.
- 63. Right foot lands on northeast diagonal in right rear stance, twin downward palm heel block. (wrists touching)

3
- 64. Left jump reverse side kick to northeast. Land in left sparring stance to northeast with right foot remaining in place. Kihap.
- 65. Right foot steps 1 sparring stance length northeast, left spin heel kick to northeast, Land in middle stance.
- 66. Double step northeast to middle stance (right foot on north point), twin back elbow strike to rear.

---(Direction Change on Line Corner)---

6
- 67. Left foot steps to right for low closed stance to north, slow (2 seconds) twin palm heel push to sides, shoulder level.
- 68. Left foot steps counterclockwise to right rear stance to south (right foot on north point). Low right reverse inner forearm block to south. And...

WORLD TRADITIONAL TAEKWONDO UNION HEADQUARTERS
6210 Baseline Road, Little Rock, Arkansas 72209 / 501-568-4181

SOK BONG POOME-SAE
FOURTH DEGREE BLACK BELT

6
69. In a continuous motion, left downward punch.
70. Right reverse punch to south middle section. And...
71. In a continuous motion, right repeat punch to south middle section. And...
72. In a continuous motion, left punch to middle section.

8
73. Left foot steps to right, right foot steps south to left back stance (left foot on north point), right high, left low block to south with tension. (5 seconds)
74. #2 Left front kick to low or middle section. And...
75. In a continuous motion, left round kick. And...
76. In a continuous motion, left hook kick.
77. Land in left sparring stance to south, right foot steps to left for #3 left hook kick to south. And...
78. In a continuous motion, left round kick to south.
79. Land in right back stance to south (left foot on center point), right reverse augmented circular downward hammerfist strike (elbow of striking arm on back fist of other arm) to south.
80. No step, left circular downward augmented backfist strike (elbow of striking arm on back fist of other arm) to south.

4
81. Right foot steps south to middle stance (body faces east, left foot on center point). Double circle knifehand low block to north.
82. No step, circle double outer forearm low block to south.
83. No step, circle double inner forearm block to north high section.
84. No step, circle double ridgehand block to south high section.

Bah-ro - Right foot steps across to end position.

Shi-uh - At ease position

(NOTE) Since the diagonals (southeast "lines" in the form) are 12 "feet" long, stance and jumps must be the proper length to ensure the performer ends the form properly.

Copyright 1985 & 1997, American Taekwondo Association. (October 15, 1997)

Songahm Taekwondo® 사단 4th Degree Black Belt

SOK BONG

☆ June Bee - Half Command Ready Position

#		Technique	Stance	Section
1.	R	Double Knifehand Strike	X	M
2.	L	Spin Heel Kick	–	H
3.	L	Sweep	–	L
4.	L	Round Kick	–	M
5.	R	Upset Knifehand Block	K	H
6.	L	Vertical Punch	K	M
7.	B	L- Knifehand High Block,	–	H
		R- Upset Knifehand Strike	–	M
8.	L	Archand Strike	K	H
9.	R	Upward Elbow Strike	K	H
10.	R	Double Outer Forearm Block	M	H
11.	R	Downward Palmheel Block	LF	L
12.	R	Jump Side Kick	–	M/H
13.	L	C Punch	B	L&H
14.	B	Twin Upset Knifehand Strike	F	H
15.	B	Twin Knifehand Block	F	H
16.	B	Twin Punch	OL	H
17.	L	Jump Front Kick	–	H
18.	R	Jump Front Kick	–	H
19.	L	Jump Front Kick	–	H
20.	R	Tension Double Knifehand Low Block	B	L
21.	L	Tension Double Knifehand Block	B	H
22.	R	Jump Round Kick	–	H
23.	L	Spin Crescent Kick	–	H
24.	R	Double Outer Forearm Block - Kihap	B	H
25.	L	Reverse First Knuckle Upset Punch	B	H
26.	L	Reverse First Finger Strike	B	H
27.	L	#2 Inner Crescent Kick	–	H
28.	L	Inward Palm Heel Block	R	M
29.	R	Reverse Punch	R	M
30.	L	Punch	R	M
31.	R	Reverse Punch	R	M
32.	L	Double Inner Forearm Block	B	H
33.	B	High/Low Block	B	H&L
34.	B	High/Low Palm Heel Block	B	H&L
35.	R	#2 Front Kick	–	H
36.	R	Round Kick		H
37.	R	Hook Kick	–	H
38.	R	#3 Hook Kick	–	H
39.	R	Round Kick	–	H
40.	R	Upset Arc Hand Strike	B	H
41.	L	Circular Downward Hammerfist Strike	C	M
42.	L	Circular Dbl Down Knifehand Strike	B	H
43.	L	#1 Side Kick	–	H
44.	L	Tension Down Palmheel Blk - Kihap	LF	L
45.	B	Knifehand X Block	B	M
46.	R	Side Kick	–	H
47.	R	Repeat Side Kick	–	H
48.	B	L- Knifehand High Block,	K	H
		R- Vertical Ridgehand Strike	–	L
49.	L	Upset Knifehand Block	K	H
50.	R	Reverse Punch	K	M
51.	L	Punch	K	H
52.	L	Double Knifehand Strike	X	M
53.	R	Spin Heel Kick	–	H
54.	L	Slow Double Ridgehand Block	B	H
55.	B	C Block	B	M&H
56.	L	Jump Spin Heel Kick	–	H
57.	R	Double Ridgehand Block	B	H
58.	B	Slow C Block	B	M&H
59.	B	Twin Punch	OL	H
60.	R	Jump Front Kick	–	H
61.	L	Jump Front Kick	–	H
62.	R	Jump Front Kick	–	H
63.	B	Twin Downward Palm Heel Block	R	L
64.	L	Jump Reverse Side Kick - Kihap	–	M
65.	L	Spin Heel Kick	–	H
66.	B	Twin Back Elbow Strike	M	M
67.	B	Slow Twin Palm Heel Push	C	H
68.	R	Reverse Low Inner Forearm Block	R	L
69.	L	Downward Punch	R	L
70.	R	Reverse Punch	R	M
71.	R	Repeat Punch	R	M
72.	L	Punch	R	M
73.	B	Tension High/Low Block	B	H&L
74.	L	#2 Front Kick	–	H
75.	L	Round Kick	–	H
76.	L	Hook Kick	–	H
77.	L	#3 Hook Kick	–	H
78.	L	Round Kick	–	H
79.	R	Rev Augmented Cir Down Hammerfist	B	H
80.	L	Augmented Cir Downward Backfist	B	H
81.	L	Circular Double Knifehand Block	M	L
82.	R	Circular Double Outer Forearm Block	M	L
83.	L	Circular Double Inner Forearm Block	M	H
84.	R	Circular Double Ridgehand Block	M	H

Requirements

At 4th degree black belt, you are becoming a high rank in Taekwondo. When you become a Master, your form will have moves that you develop in addition to the standard form. As a 4th Degree, you will develop a "form" that will be demonstrated at the a Graduation as part of your midterm.

The requirements are:
1) It must be written and submitted to your instructor at least 3 months prior to graduation.
2) Approval must be granted before 1 month prior to graduation.
3) It may include new weapons or any materials.
4) It must have some philosophical justification (i.e. WHY is it being done?, WHAT significance does it have or relate to?).
5) You must turn in the following 2 pages.

My 4° Creative Form:

Include all weapons, props, people required, or materials. It should be a complete description.

Master Club Curriculum - 4° ProTech

My 4° Creative Form: Announcement

This is for the MC at the Graduation to read to describe your creative form to the audience. Please include all philosophy and physical explanation. Also include when they should speak or any other instructions (ex: "When the music starts, say this____")

 *Master Club Curriculum - 4° ProTech*

4° Application

This must be sent in to the ATA 6 months (or more) prior to testing for 5° Black Belt. This is included for reference and subject to change. Verify you are using the most up to date form with your instructor.

ATA / STF / WTTU International HQ
PO Box 193010, Little Rock, AR 72219
Inst. Dept. Ext. 2268: Fax Number: 866-423-5430

Updated 12/23/2013

HIGH RANK MIDTERM & TESTING CHECKLIST

High Rank = those <u>presently holding</u> the rank of 4th Degree Black Belt or Higher!

Application must be submitted 6 months in advance of participating in Rank Testing

Midterm:
Page 2 of the following application should be sent to ATA HQ 30 days in advance of the event you wish to midterm at. Midterms are subject to denial.

Rank Test:
1. Initial high rank test must be completed at a World event.
2. Complete pages 2-3 of the application following this checklist. Send it to ATA HQ with a DVD presentation of your TKD Form. **It <u>must be</u> received at ATA Headquarters 6 months in advance of the event you wish to test at (no excuses accepted!).**
3. All other requirements must be completed and received at headquarters no later than 30 days in advance of the event date, or an individual will be dropped from the testing roster.
4. Approval / denial letters will be sent out no later than 30 days prior to the date of the event.
5. **If a no change** is received, high rank applicants may re-test at Fall or Spring Nationals or a World Championship event.

Midterm Requirements:
- Signature of Senior Instructor must be <u>on</u> application prior to mailing to HQ
- ATA Fit Test will be part of the testing event
- Payment in full enclosed with application (4th = $135, 5th = $165, 6th = $150, 7th & 8th = NA)

Rank Test Requirements:
- Signature of Senior Instructor must be <u>on</u> application prior to mailing to HQ
- DVD presentation of your Taekwondo Form
- Time in Rank must be complete prior to testing
- Mid-Terms must be complete (and in house at HQ no later than 30 days prior to the event) 7th degree and 8th Degree - no midterms required
- Payment in full enclosed with application (less mid-term fees paid)
  Test fees: 4th = $400, 5th = $500, 6th = $600, 7th = $700, 8th = $800
- Instructor Status – Certified Instructor (black collar)
- Certification must be current (no later than 30 days prior to the event!)
- ATA Fit Test will be part of the testing event
- Regional Participation
- Licensees   Testing results sent to HQ Pd in full and up-to-date
  ATA account must be paid in full
  WMA account must be paid in full
- Leadership Points – *See page 4-5 of this High Rank Testing Application for details*
- Accredited National Participation – *See page 6 of this High Rank Testing Application for details.*

h/tsh/testing/appsasofsep08/test&midapphighrankmay13.doc

ATA / STF / WTTU International HQ
PO Box 193010, Little Rock, AR 72219
Inst. Dept. Ext. 2268: Fax Number: 866-423-5430

HIGH RANK MIDTERM & TESTING APPLICATION
HIGH RANKS – those presently holding the rank of 4th Degree or higher (12/23/2013)

<u>Midterms:</u> <u>Page 2</u> of this application along with appropriate fees should be sent to ATA HQ 30 days in advance of the date you wish to midterm. Midterm applicants are subject to denial.

<u>Rank Test:</u> Initial testing must be completed at a World Championship event. Complete <u>pages 2 – 3</u> of this application and submit to ATA HQ with a **DVD presentation of your TKD Form** at least **SIX MONTHS prior to the date of the event.** Please note that applications may be denied. **Applicants will be denied if all requirements are not complete within 30 days of the event. FINAL approvals/denials will be made no later than 30 days prior to the event date.**

My Email Address is:_____

I wish to: Midterm __   Rank Test __   At (event/date/location): _____

Name _____Age _____ Birth Date _____

ATA # _____ Rank (I am) _____ Date of Rank _____ Inst. #_____

Address correspondence is to be sent to: _____
City_____ State/Country _____ Zip _____

Home Phone (____) _____ Cell/alternate Phone (____) _____

My Instructor's name is: _____
My School Owners name is: _____

Physical material approved by my Instructor: The **3** items I will perform are -
    TKD Form __   Free Spar __   Board Breaks __   Protech __
        Boards - consisting of _____
        Protech topic _____

Amount enclosed $_____

My senior's signature and a DVD presentation of myTKD form IS INCLUDED with this application! I authorize investigation of all statements contained in this application. I understand that misrepresentation or omission of facts called for is cause for rejection of application. I understand that if I do not get my seniors approval and permission to test or midterm, I shall be denied by ATA HQ. I understand that I must have my senior's signature of approval PRIOR to applying to ATA HQ.   **Senior's Signature denotes approval. Do not sign if not approved.**

_____   _____
Applicants Signature   **Date**   **Senior Instructor's Signature**   **Date**

ATA / STF / WTTU International HQ
PO Box 193010, Little Rock, AR 72219
Inst. Dept. Ext. 2268: Fax Number: 866-423-5430

12/23/2013

Leadership Points are required for rank test applicants who <u>ARE</u> 4th degree or higher: Due to the fact that this requirement became mandatory, with NO grandfather clause, **each applicant must** compare their personal records to the records on his/her member file online. Attach a separate sheet to this application with the following information (or email an <u>excel</u> file to melanie.morris@ataonline.com): *See pages 4 – 5 of this High Rank Test application for details.*

Name of topic	Date	Location	Host	Instructor of topic

Instructor Status: Certified (black collar) required to test for the rank of 5th degree or above!
    Date Certified: _____ Expire Date _____
       Re-certification <u>must be completed</u> 30 days prior to the event.

Midterms: Dates and Locations:

_____   _____
_____   _____

Accredited National Participation - topic/dates: *See page 6 of this application for details*

_____   _____
_____   _____
_____   _____
_____   _____

If not a school or club owner, at whose facility do you teach or manage?
Name: _____ Location _____ School # _____
Name: _____ Location _____ School # _____

School/Club Owner: Licensed facilities you have owned (if extra space is needed, attach additional pages)
#_____ Location _____ Date: from – to _____ Avg. # testing _____
#_____ Location _____ Date: from – to _____ Avg. # testing _____
#_____ Location _____ Date: from – to _____ Avg. # testing _____

Your Junior Instructors who own schools or clubs: (if extra space is needed, attach additional pages)
Name _____ #_____ Location _____
Name _____ #_____ Location _____
Name _____ #_____ Location _____

FOR HQ OFFICE USE ONLY:
Date App Received _____ DVD Received _____ Training Instructor/Senior of Record Approval _____ _____
Pd $_____ Paid Via & date _____ Licensee – Account Information:
Rank _____ Time in Rank _____ Status: ATA _____ WMA _____
Age Req. _____ Numbers: Test/New _____ Testing Results: _____

h/tsh/testing/appsasofsep08/test&midapphighrankmay13.doc

ATA / STF / WTTU International HQ
PO Box 193010, Little Rock, AR 72219
Inst. Dept. Ext. 2268: Fax Number: 866-423-5430

12/23/2013 this sheet supersedes any previously dated or undated material regarding testing requirements. (First adopted 2/9/05)

TESTING REQUIREMENT:
Leadership Points / Accredited National Participation / Titles
(Testing <u>for</u> the rank of 5th Degree <u>and Above</u>)

Leadership Credit points can be obtained through a combination of the following;

Testing numbers	Instruction Seminars (hosted by HQ)
New member numbers	Business Seminars (hosted by HQ)
Tournament judging	Protech Certification/Camp (hosted by HQ)
Regional Testing guest judging	Overseas activities (hosted by HQ)
National Camp participation	Program/Material development (via HQ)

** There IS NO Grandfather clause – individuals will not receive permission to test
until the total required leadership credit points for their rank has been achieved.

These credit points should be accumulated throughout the "time-in-rank" requirement;

4th Degree Black Belt = 360 points (90 credits per year for 4 years).
5th Degree Black Belt = 450 points (90 credits per year for 5 years).
6th Degree Black Belt = 540 points (90 credits per year for 6 years).
7th Degree Black Belt = 630 points (90 credits per year for 7 years).
8t^{h} Degree Black Belt = 720 points (90 credits per year for 8 years).

I. **Leadership Point Accumulation**

    A. Numbers (are tabulated from the last full year prior to testing date)

4DB 100 new members or a test number average of	100
5DB 300 new members or a test number average of	300
6DB 1000 new members or a test number average of	1000
7DB 3000 new members or a test number average of	3000
8DB 6000 new members or a test number average of	6000

Meeting 10% of required numbers =	5 Leader points per year time in rank
Meeting 20% of required numbers =	10 Leader points per year time in rank
Meeting 30% of required numbers =	15 Leader points per year time in rank
Meeting 40% of required numbers =	20 Leader points per year time in rank
Meeting 50% of required numbers =	25 Leader points per year time in rank
Meeting 60% of required numbers =	30 Leader points per year time in rank
Meeting 70% of required numbers =	35 Leader points per year time in rank
Meeting 80% of required numbers =	40 Leader points per year time in rank
Meeting 100% of required numbers =	50 Leaders Points per year time in rank

ATA / STF / WTTU International HQ
PO Box 193010, Little Rock, AR 72219
Inst. Dept. Ext. 2268: Fax Number: 866-423-5430

12/23/2013

B. Leadership Credit Points: Tournament Judging or Staff
- 1 Point — Per Ring Judged at Regional's – Max 20 per year
- 2 Points — Per Ring Judged at Nationals – Max 14 per year
- 3 Points — Per Ring Judged at Worlds– Max 12 per year

** Make sure to put your ATA Number on all tournament ring packets next to your name!

C. Leadership Points: Personal Improvement / Leadership Activities
- 15 Points — Leadership Camp
- 15 Points — Protech Camp
- 15 Points — Korea Trips hosted by HQ
- 10 Points — National Instructor Certification Upgrade/Re-cert Camps
- 5 Points — World Conference Topics
- 5 Points — Regional Camps/Seminars - Max 20 points per year
- 5 Points — Instruction Seminars – Max 20 points per year
- 5 Points — Business Seminars - Maximum 20 points per year
- 5 Points — Protech Seminars - Maximum 20 points per year
- 5 Points — MASS Training Seminar – Maximum 10 points per year

D. Leadership Points: Regional Testing Guest Judge
- 5 Points — Guest Judge at a regional test – Max 20 points per year
  ** Make sure to keep your own records of dates and locations!

E. Leadership Points: Contributions to Organization / Community Participation
- 10 Points — Development of new programs/material
- 10 Points — Community Work/Contribution

F. Personal Improvement Seminars (Krav Maga, Leadership, etc.)
At this time points will not be awarded however, these "other" seminars may be taken into consideration by the Grand Master in making his final decision towards approval.

Note 1: Individuals must achieve their required point total within their "time-in-rank". If they fall short, at the end of their required time in rank minimum, they must wait the extra year or years it takes to reach the required total for their rank.

Note 2: To test, individuals do not have to acquire points in testing or new member numbers, they can make up the numbers by achieving points in other activities.

ATA / STF / WTTU International HQ
PO Box 193010, Little Rock, AR 72219
Inst. Dept. Ext. 2268: Fax Number: 866-423-5430

12/23/2013

II. Accredited National Training Participation:

All Black Belts age 18 years and up, who attain the rank of 3rd Degree Black Belt through 7th Degree Black Belt as of January 1, 2013 and after, are required to participate in Accredited National Leadership Training Activities.

Accredited National Leadership Training Activities are:
World Conference (part of World Expo)
HQ Leadership Camp / Songahm Training Camp
HQ Protech Camp
HQ Korea Trips
Jacksonville Master's Gathering

The amount/number breakdown, by rank, is as follows:
3rd Degree - 1
4th Degree - 2
5th Degree - 5
6th Degree - 6
7th Degree - 7

III. Testing VS Title consideration

See the Testing Application for requirements needed to receive testing approval. These requirements are different from the Mastership Title process.

There are 3 stages to the Mastership Process.
    a. Candidate status is achieved when appropriate rank is awarded.
    b. Nominee status is achieved via these initial requirements & official invitation
        i. Numbers – Testing average OR New Members
            Master Title   200
            Sr. Master Title   500
            Ch. Master Title   1000
        ii. OR – National Leadership Training Participation
            Master Title   9 (combined 4th – 5th degree participation)
            Sr. Master   6 (6th degree participation)
            Ch Master   7 (7th degree participation)
        iii. Owners Must
            Have all in-school testing results up-to-date & paid in full
            Have all accounts paid in full (ATA/STF/WTTU & WMA)
    c. Inductee status is achieved when all nominee application requirements are met.

My Notes on My Road to Master

My Notes on My Road to Master

Master Club

5° Black Belt Curriculum

ATA

BLACK BELT ACADEMY

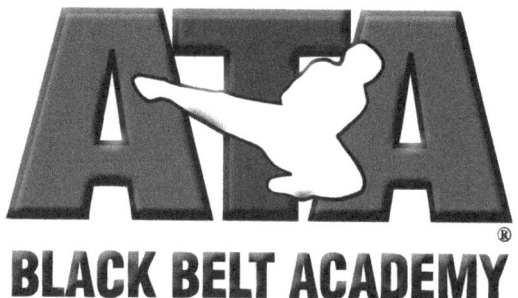

5° Black Belt to 6° Black Belt Rank Requirements:

As a 5° Black Belt, you are now on your final steps to Master. 6° is only one step - following the achievement of this high rank you must train at least a year and be accepted as a Master Candidate. You must start attending ATA leadership camp and working on meeting the strict requirements of Mastership. Your training now changes to becoming a leader at a school or schools. See the following pages for application information. You will get some required materials sent to you through the ATA.

My Road to Mastery!

6° Black Belt Planner:

Take a minute and plan your road to 6° black belt. Your instructor can help you find the correct dates. At 5°, you should plan on midterming 3 times, PLUS Supplemental Demonstrations at the Black Belt Graduations at least once per year.

Current Rank	Testing For:	Requirements:	Graduation Fee:*	My Grad Date
4°	5°	Successful Testing at World Championships, Sok Bong, Board Breaks at Graduation, Sparring, Current 4° ProTech Requirements **Testing Must be Done at World Championships**	ATA Fee (at School)	__/__/__
5°	Midterm#1	12-24 Months, Chung Hae, Board Breaks, Sparring, Current 4° ProTech Requirements (at School) **Midterm Must be Done at National Event**	ATA Fee	__/__/__
5°	Midterm#2	24-36 Months at Rank, Chung Hae, Board Breaks, Board Breaks, Current 4° ProTech Requirements (at School) **Midterm Must be Done at National Event**	ATA Fee	__/__/__
5°	Midterm#3	36-48 Months at Rank, Chung Hae, Board Breaks, Sparring, Current 4° ProTech Requirements (at School) **Midterm Must be Done at National Event**	ATA Fee	__/__/__
4°	5°	60 Months at Rank, Chung Hae, Board Breaks at Graduation, Sparring, **Current Certified Instructor, ATA Application Accepted** (see online for Application) **Testing Must be Done at World Championships**	ATA Fee	

*Graduation fees and requirements subject to change.

Rev 4.0 - © KarateBuilt L.L.C.

Master Club 5° Black Belt
ProTech Material Rotation

Type	Even Years			Odd Years		
	March Graduation	July Graduation	November Graduation	March Graduation	July Graduation	November Graduation
Regular	Creative	Long Range Jahng Bong	Jee Pahng Ee	Gumdo	Mid Range Jahng Bong	Sahm Dahm Bong
Supplemental	1° BME Form	1° SJB Form	2° Ssahng Nat Form	2° DSJB Form	2° DBME Form	1° Knife Form

*Supplemental material is for in-class training. While not a primary requirement for testing/midterms 5° and up students are responsible for all lower rank material.

Required Equipment – Same as 3°*

* For your safety, all equipment must be American Taekwondo Association / ProTech approved
** Creative Form if required must be approved by instructor

My Notes on My Road to Master

CHUNGHAE POOME-SAE
FIFTH DEGREE BLACK BELT

Translates as "Mastered all kinds of knowledge and utilizes this to do many things."

NEW STANCE: Short front stance. [15, 16, 92, 93]

NEW BLOCKS: Reverse inward hammerfist block. [1]
Upper pressing block. [49, 79]
Twin palm block. [34, 64]
Twin pressing block. [53, 57]

NEW STRIKES: Bow wrist strike. [15, 92]
Double hammerfist strike. [43, 73]

NEW KICKS: Stomping kick. [47, 77]
Step jump spin hook kick. [17, 94]
Step jump spin outer crescent kick. [22, 27]
#3 Jump spin outer crescent kick. [51, 55]
Hooking sweep. [44, 74]

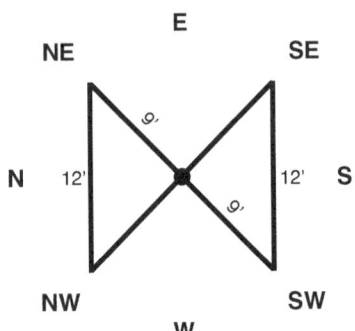

NEW PREPARATION TECHNIQUE: One fist retracts to rib cage; other fist crosses chest at shoulder level, fist held palm down. [42, 72]

Form should take about 2:10 to 2:15 minutes from attention to final bow
All advanced open hand techniques begin in a closed hand position (fist)

READY STANCE: *Full command stance; left foot steps to parallel stance, left arm is inside right; hands are in knifehand position.*

☆ June Bee - Full command stance.

3
1. Left foot triple steps northwest to right front stance to southeast, left reverse inward hammerfist block to middle section. (Left foot steps northwest ½ stance length, right foot steps past left a further ½ stance length, then left steps past right to form right front stance. Right foot is one stance length from center point).
2. No step, right punch to high section.
3. No step, left reverse punch to middle section.

6
4. Left foot double steps southeast to right front stance, high knifehand X-block to southeast. (In double step, left foot comes to parallel stance, then right foot steps back to front stance, right foot on center point).
5. #2 left front kick to southeast. And...
6. In a continuous motion, left back kick to northwest. (Middle or High)
7. Land in right back stance to northwest, circle low double knifehand low block to northwest.
8. Double step northwest to middle stance, circle double knifehand strike to northwest middle section.
9. No step, circle square block to northwest.

CHUNGHAE POOME-SAE
FIFTH DEGREE BLACK BELT

7
10. Left foot pulls back to parallel stance, left outer forearm pressing block to northwest.
11. Turning counter clockwise, left foot steps southeast to middle stance (left foot on center point), right inner forearm low block to northwest.
12. #3 right side kick to northwest. (Middle or High) And...
13. In a fast, continuous motion, right hook kick to northwest. (Middle or High) And...
14. In a fast, continuous motion, right round kick to northwest. (Middle or High)
15. Land in right short front stance (½ front stance) to northwest, right bow wrist strike to northwest high section.
16. No step, left reverse palm heel strike to northwest high section.

4
17. Left foot steps northwest ½ short front stance length past right for right jump spin hook kick to northwest.
18. Land in right back stance to northwest, (cross arms only ½ way for preparation) advanced low double outer forearm block to northwest.
19. Face southeast; shift in place to left back stance, slow circle double inner forearm block to southeast middle section.
20. Moving the right foot, shift to a long stance, slow circle double low knifehand block to southeast.

5
21. Right foot draws back to left foot, then steps southeast one sparring stance length; left foot steps southeast one sparring stance length; #3 left jump front kick to southeast (right foot will land two stance lengths from where foot takes off, on center point).
22. Left foot lands to southeast in left sparring stance, right foot steps forward ½ stance length for left jump spin outer crescent kick to southeast.
23. Land in right sparring stance to southeast; right foot steps behind left to left X-stance, advanced double knifehand block to southeast middle section.
24. Left foot steps northwest to left back stance to southeast; advanced double outer forearm block to southeast middle section.
25. Turning clockwise, right foot steps northwest to right back stance, advanced double knifehand block to southeast middle section (left foot on center point). <u>Kihap</u>.

5
26. Left foot draws back to right foot, then steps southeast one sparring stance length, right foot steps southeast one sparring stance length; #3 right jump front kick to southeast (left foot will land two stance lengths from where foot takes off).
27. Right foot lands to southeast in right sparring stance, left foot steps forward ½ stance length (to southeast point) for right jump spin outer crescent kick to southeast.
28. Land in middle stance, X-knifehand low block to southwest.
29. Shift in place to right back stance, slow circle double inner forearm block to southeast middle section.
30. Moving the right foot, shift to a long stance, slow circle double low knifehand block to southeast.

---(Direction Change on Line Corner)---

AMERICAN TAEKWONDO ASSOCIATION HEADQUARTERS
6210 Baseline Road, Little Rock, Arkansas 72209 / 501-568-2821

CHUNGHAE POOME-SAE
FIFTH DEGREE BLACK BELT

12
31. Right foot steps to left foot (to southeast point), turning counter clockwise, left foot steps west to right rear stance, advanced double inner forearm block to west middle section.
32. Left foot steps west to right back stance, left punch to west high section.
33. No step, right reverse upset punch to west middle section.
34. Right foot steps west one sparring stance length, left foot steps behind to right X-stance (south side center point), high twin palm block to west.
35. Left foot steps east to middle stance, right ridgehand strike to west high section.
36. Left foot steps behind right to right X-stance, right circle hammerfist strike to west middle section.
37. No step, face east; circle knifehand square block to east.
38. Pivoting counterclockwise in place (lift both heels) to left X-stance to west, left advanced double knifehand block to west middle section.
39. Right foot steps west in front of left foot to right X-stance, right low double knifehand block to east low section.
40. Right side kick to east. (High or Middle)
41. Turning counter clockwise, right foot lands in middle stance to west (left foot on south center side point), left spin heel kick to west.
42. Left foot lands to east in middle stance (left foot on south center side point). Left fist moves (slow) to left rib cage, as right forearm moves (slow) to horizontal position in front of chest with hammerfist down (palm facing body, five (5) inches away).

8
43. Double step west to middle stance (right foot on southwest point), circle double hammerfist strike to west middle section.
44. Right hooking sweep moving into left X-stance.
45. Right reverse ridgehand strike downward from left X-stance (as to fallen opponent). Kihap.
46. No step, left downward punch (as to fallen opponent).
47. #2 right stomping kick to west (as to fallen opponent). Right foot steps down to west ½ stance length (as though stepping over fallen opponent, left foot on southwest point). Left foot skips into left one leg stance in preparation for...
48. Right side kick to east low section (as to fallen opponent). Right foot retracts.

---(Direction Change on Line Corner)---

49. Right upper pressing block to northeast in left one leg stance.
50. No step, look southwest for left reinforced inner forearm block to west middle section.

3
51. Right foot steps northeast one sparring stance length, left foot steps northeast one sparring stance length for left #3 jump spin outer crescent kick to southwest. Land in middle stance. (Right foot lands on center point, body facing southeast).
52. Turning counter clockwise, right jump reverse inner crescent kick to southwest. (Left foot gains 1½ sparring stance lengths; left foot lands ½ stance southwest of center point).
53. Land in middle stance; twin pressing block to low section. (Right hand to right side; left hand to front of body).

CHUNGHAE POOME-SAE
FIFTH DEGREE BLACK BELT

4
54. Left foot lifts to right knee cap; right reinforced inner forearm block to southwest middle section.
55. Left foot steps northeast one sparring stance length, right foot steps northeast one sparring stance length for right #3 jump spin outer crescent kick to southwest. Land in middle stance (body facing northwest).
56. Turning clockwise, left jump reverse inner crescent kick to southwest. (Right foot gains 1½ sparring stance lengths).
57. Land in middle stance; (left foot on center point) twin pressing block to low section. (Left hand to left side, right hand to front of body).

3
58. Left foot steps northeast past right foot to right X-stance, left advanced double knifehand block to southwest middle section.
59. Right foot steps northeast to right back stance, advanced double outer forearm block to southwest middle section.
60. Left foot steps northeast to left back stance, (left foot on northeast point) advanced double knifehand block to southwest middle section.

---(Direction Change on Line Corner)---

12
61. Right foot steps to east-west line to left rear stance, advanced double inner forearm block to west middle section.
62. Right foot steps west to left back stance, right punch to west high section.
63. No step, left reverse upset punch to west middle section.
64. Left foot steps west one sparring stance length, right foot steps behind to left X-stance, (north side center point) high twin palm block to west.
65. Right foot steps east to middle stance, left ridgehand strike to west high section. <u>Kihap</u>.
66. Right foot steps behind left to left X-stance, left circle hammerfist strike to west middle section.
67. No step, face east; circle knifehand square block to east.
68. Pivoting clockwise in place (lift both heels) to right X-stance to west, right advanced double knifehand block to west middle section.
69. Left foot steps west in front of right foot to left X-stance, left low double knifehand block to east low section.
70. Left side kick to east. (Middle or High)
71. Turning clockwise, left foot lands in middle stance to west, right spin heel kick to west.
72. Right foot lands to east in middle stance. Right fist moves (slow) to right rib cage, as left forearm moves (slow) to horizontal position in front of chest with hammerfist down (palm facing body, five (5) inches away).

8
73. Double step west to middle stance (left foot on northwest point), circle double hammerfist strike to west middle section.
74. Left hooking sweep moving into right X-stance.
75. Left reverse ridgehand strike downward from right X-stance (as to fallen opponent).
76. No step, right downward punch (as to fallen opponent).

CHUNGHAE POOME-SAE
FIFTH DEGREE BLACK BELT

8
77. #2 left stomping kick to west (as to fallen opponent). Left foot steps down to west ½ stance length (as though stepping over fallen opponent, right foot on northwest point). Right foot skips into right one leg stance in preparation for...
78. Left side kick to east low section (as to fallen opponent). Left foot retracts.

---(Direction Change on Line Corner)---

79. Left upper pressing block to southeast in right one leg stance.
80. No step, right outer forearm block to northwest middle section.

6
81. Left foot steps down to southeast in right back stance, high knifehand X-block to southeast.
82. #2 right front kick to southeast. And...
83. In a continuous motion, right back kick to northwest. (Middle or High)
84. Land in left back stance to southeast, circle low double knifehand low block to southeast.
85. Double step southeast to middle stance (right foot on center point), circle double knifehand strike to southeast middle section. <u>Kihap</u>.
86. No step, circle square block to southeast.

7
87. Right foot pulls back to parallel stance, right outer forearm pressing block to southeast.
88. Turning clockwise, right foot steps northwest to middle stance, left inner forearm low block to southeast.
89. #3 left side kick to southeast. (Middle or High) And...
90. In a fast, continuous motion, left hook kick to southeast. (Middle or High) And...
91. In a fast, continuous motion, left round kick to southeast. (Middle or High)
92. Land in left short front stance (½ front stance) to southeast, left bow wrist strike to southeast high section.
93. No step, right reverse palm heel strike to southeast high section.

2
94. Right foot steps southeast to ½ short front stance length past left (to center point) for left jump spin hook kick to southeast.
95. Land in left back stance (right foot on center point) to southeast, (cross arms only ½ way for preparation) advanced low double outer forearm block to southeast.

Bah-ro - Left foot steps to ready position.

Shi-uh - At ease position.

Copyright 1985, 1986 & 1996, American Taekwondo Association. (October 24, 1996)

CHUNGHAE

Songahm Taekwondo®   오단   5th Degree Black Belt

☆ June Bee - Full Command Ready Position

#		Technique	Stance	Section
1.	L	Reverse Inward Hammerfist Block	F	M
2.	R	Punch	F	H
3.	L	Reverse Punch	F	M
4.	B	High Knifehand X-Block	F	H
5.	L	#2 Front Kick	--	H
6.	L	Back Kick	--	M/H
7.	L	Circular Double Knifehand Block	B	L
8.	L	Circular Double Knifehand Strike	M	M
9.	B	Circle Square Block	M	M&H
10.	L	Outer Forearm Pressing Block	P	L
11.	R	Inner Forearm Low Block	M	L
12.	R	#3 Side Kick	--	M/H
13.	R	Hook Kick	--	M/H
14.	R	Round Kick	--	M/H
15.	R	Bow Wrist Strike	1/2F	H
16.	L	Reverse Palm Heel Strike	1/2F	H
17.	R	Jump Spin Hook Kick	--	H
18.	L	Advanced Low Double Outer Forearm Block	B	L
19.	R	Slow Circular Double Inner Forearm Block	B	M
20.	R	Slow Circular Double Low Knifehand Block	L	L
21.	L	#3 Jump Front Kick	--	H
22.	L	Jump Spin Outer Crescent Kick	--	H
23.	R	Advanced Double Knifehand Block	X	M
24.	R	Advanced Double Outer Forearm Block	B	M
25.	L	Advanced Double Knifehand Block - Kihap	B	M
26.	R	#3 Jump Front Kick	--	M/H
27.	R	Jump Spin Outer Crescent Kick	--	M/H
28.	B	Low X-Knifehand Block	M	L
29.	L	Slow Circular Double Inner Forearm Block	B	M
30.	L	Slow Circular Low Double Knifehand Block	L	L
31.	L	Advanced Double Inner Forearm Block	R	M
32.	L	Punch	B	H
33.	R	Reverse Upset Punch	B	M
34.	B	High Twin Palm Block	X	H
35.	R	Ridgehand Strike	M	H
36.	R	Circular Hammerfist Strike	X	M
37.	B	Circular Knifehand Square Block	X	M&H
38.	L	Advanced Double Knifehand Block	X	M
39.	R	Double Low Knifehand Block	X	L
40.	R	Side Kick	--	M/H
41.	L	Spin Heel Kick	--	H
42.	B	L- Fist to Hip, R- Vertical Punch	M	M
43.	R	Circular Double Hammerfist Strike	M	M
44.	R	Hooking Sweep	X	L
45.	R	Reverse Down Ridgehand Strike - Kihap	X	L
46.	L	Downward Punch	X	L
47.	R	#2 Stomping Kick	--	L
48.	R	Side Kick	--	L
49.	R	Upper Pressing Block	OL	H
50.	L	Reinforced Inner Forearm Block	OL	M
51.	L	#3 Jump Spin Outer Crescent Kick	--	M
52.	R	Jump Reverse Inner Crescent Kick	--	H
53.	B	Twin Pressing Block	M	L
54.	R	Reinforced Inner Forearm Block	OL	M
55.	R	#3 Jump Spin Outer Crescent Kick	--	H
56.	L	Jump reverse Inner Crescent Kick	--	H
57.	B	Twin Pressing Block	M	L
58.	L	Advanced Double Knifehand Block	X	M
59.	L	Advanced Double Outer Forearm Block	B	M
60.	R	Advanced Double Knifehand Block	B	M
61.	R	Advanced Double Inner Forearm Block	R	M
62.	R	Punch	B	H
63.	L	Reverse Upset Punch	B	M
64.	B	High Twin Palm Block	X	H
65.	L	Ridgehand Strike - Kihap	M	H
66.	L	Circular Hammerfist Strike	X	M
67.	B	Circular Knifehand Square Block	X	M&H
68.	R	Advanced Double Knifehand Block	X	M
69.	L	Double Low Knifehand Block	X	L
70.	L	Side Kick	--	M/H
71.	R	Spin Heel Kick	--	H
72.	B	R- Fist to Hip, L- Vertical Punch	M	M
73.	L	Circular Double Hammerfist Strike	M	M
74.	L	Hooking Sweep	X	L
75.	L	Reverse Downward Ridgehand Strike	X	L
76.	R	Downward Punch	X	L
77.	L	#2 Stomping Kick	--	L
78.	L	Side Kick	--	L
79.	L	Upper Pressing Block	OL	H
80.	R	Outer Forearm Block	OL	M
81.	B	High Knifehand X-Block	B	H
82.	R	#2 Front Kick	--	H
83.	R	Back Kick	--	M/H
84.	R	Low Circular Double Knifehand Block	B	L
85.	R	Circular Double Knifehand Strike - Kihap	M	M
86.	B	Circular Square Block	M	M&H
87.	R	Outer Forearm Pressing Block	P	L
88.	L	Inner Forearm Low Block	M	L
89.	L	#3 Side Kick	--	M/H
90.	L	Hook Kick	--	M/H
91.	L	Round Kick	--	M/H
92.	L	Bow Wrist Strike	1/2F	H
93.	R	Reverse Palm Heel Strike	1/2F	H
94.	L	Jump Spin Hook Kick	--	H
95.	L	Advanced Double Outer Forearm Block	B	L

Master Club Curriculum - 5° ProTech

My 5° Creative Form: Announcement

This is for the MC at the Graduation to read to describe your creative form to the audience. Please include all philosophy and physical explanation. Also include when they should speak or any other instructions (ex: "When the music starts, say this_____")

Master Club Curriculum - 5° ProTech

Requirements

At 5th degree black belt, you are becoming a high rank in Taekwondo. When you become a Master, your form will have moves that you develop in addition to the standard form. As a 5th Degree, you will develop a "form" that will be demonstrated at the May Graduation as part of your midterm.

The requirements are:
1) It must be written and submitted to your instructor at least 3 months prior to graduation.
2) Approval must be granted before 1 month prior to graduation.
3) It may include new weapons or any materials.
4) It must have some philosophical justification (i.e. WHY is it being done?, WHAT significance does it have or relate to?).
5) You must turn in the following 2 pages.

Master Club Curriculum - 5° ProTech

My 5° Creative Form:

Include all weapons, props, people required, or materials. It should be a complete description.

5° Application

This must be sent in to the ATA 6 months (or more) prior to testing for 6° (or higher) Black Belt. This is included for reference and subject to change. Verify you are using the most up to date form with your instructor.

ATA / STF / WTTU International HQ
PO Box 193010, Little Rock, AR 72219
Inst. Dept. Ext. 2268: Fax Number: 866-423-5430

Updated 12/23/2013

HIGH RANK MIDTERM & TESTING CHECKLIST

High Rank = those <u>presently holding</u> the rank of **4th Degree Black Belt or Higher!**

Application must be submitted 6 months in advance of participating in Rank Testing

Midterm:
Page 2 of the following application should be sent to ATA HQ 30 days in advance of the event you wish to midterm at. Midterms are subject to denial.

Rank Test:
1. Initial high rank test must be completed at a World event.
2. Complete pages 2-3 of the application following this checklist. Send it to ATA HQ with a DVD presentation of your TKD Form. **It must be received at ATA Headquarters 6 months in advance of the event you wish to test at (no excuses accepted!).**
3. All other requirements must be completed and received at headquarters no later than 30 days in advance of the event date, or an individual will be dropped from the testing roster.
4. Approval / denial letters will be sent out no later than 30 days prior to the date of the event.
5. **If a no change** is received, high rank applicants may re-test at Fall or Spring Nationals or a World Championship event.

Midterm Requirements:
- Signature of Senior Instructor must be <u>on</u> application prior to mailing to HQ
- ATA Fit Test will be part of the testing event
- Payment in full enclosed with application (4th = $135, 5th = $165, 6th = $150, 7th & 8th = NA)

Rank Test Requirements:
- Signature of Senior Instructor must be <u>on</u> application prior to mailing to HQ
- DVD presentation of your Taekwondo Form
- Time in Rank must be complete prior to testing
- Mid-Terms must be complete (and in house at HQ no later than 30 days prior to the event) 7th degree and 8th Degree - no midterms required
- Payment in full enclosed with application (less mid-term fees paid)
  Test fees: 4th = $400, 5th = $500, 6th = $600, 7th = $700, 8th = $800
- Instructor Status – Certified Instructor (black collar)
- Certification must be current (no later than 30 days prior to the event!)
- ATA Fit Test will be part of the testing event
- Regional Participation
- Licensees   Testing results sent to HQ Pd in full and up-to-date
                      ATA account must be paid in full
                      WMA account must be paid in full
- Leadership Points – *See page 4-5 of this High Rank Testing Application for details*
- Accredited National Participation – *See page 6 of this High Rank Testing Application for details.*

h/tsh/testing/appsasofsep08/test&midapphighrankmay13.doc

ATA / STF / WTTU International HQ
PO Box 193010, Little Rock, AR 72219
Inst. Dept. Ext. 2268: Fax Number: 866-423-5430

HIGH RANK MIDTERM & TESTING APPLICATION
HIGH RANKS – those presently holding the rank of 4th Degree or higher   (12/23/2013)

<u>Midterms:</u> <u>Page 2</u> of this application along with appropriate fees should be sent to ATA HQ 30 days in advance of the date you wish to midterm. Midterm applicants are subject to denial.

<u>Rank Test:</u> Initial testing must be completed at a World Championship event. Complete <u>pages 2 – 3</u> of this application and <u>submit to ATA HQ</u> with a **DVD presentation of your TKD Form** at least **SIX MONTHS** prior to the date of the event. Please note that applications may be denied. **Applicants will be denied if all requirements are not complete within 30 days of the event. FINAL approvals/denials will be made no later than 30 days prior to the event date.**

My Email Address is:_____

I wish to: Midterm __   Rank Test __   At (event/date/location): _____

Name _____ Age _____ Birth Date _____

ATA # _____ Rank (I am) _____ Date of Rank _____ Inst. # _____

Address correspondence is to be sent to: _____
City_____ State/Country _____ Zip _____

Home Phone (____) _____ Cell/alternate Phone (____) _____

My Instructor's name is: _____
My School Owners name is: _____

Physical material approved by my Instructor: The <u>3</u> items I will perform are -
    TKD Form __   *Free Spar* __   *Board Breaks* __   *Protech* __
        Boards - consisting of _____
        Protech topic _____

Amount enclosed $_____

My senior's signature and a DVD presentation of myTKD form **IS INCLUDED** with this application! I authorize investigation of all statements contained in this application. I understand that misrepresentation or omission of facts called for is cause for rejection of application. I understand that if I do not get my seniors approval and permission to test or midterm, I shall be denied by ATA HQ. I understand that I must have my senior's signature of approval PRIOR to applying to ATA HQ.   **Senior's Signature denotes approval. Do not sign if not approved.**

_____ _____   _____ _____
Applicants Signature   **Date**   **Senior Instructor's Signature**   **Date**

ATA / STF / WTTU International HQ
PO Box 193010, Little Rock, AR 72219
Inst. Dept. Ext. 2268: Fax Number: 866-423-5430

12/23/2013

Leadership Points are required for rank test applicants who <u>ARE</u> 4th degree or higher: Due to the fact that this requirement became mandatory, with NO grandfather clause, **each applicant must** compare their personal records to the records on his/her member file online. Attach a separate sheet to this application with the following information (or email an <u>excel</u> file to melanie.morris@ataonline.com): *See pages 4 – 5 of this High Rank Test application for details.*

| Name of topic | Date | Location | Host | Instructor of topic |

Instructor Status: Certified (black collar) required to test for the rank of 5th degree or above!
Date Certified: _____   Expire Date _____
Re-certification <u>must be completed</u> 30 days prior to the event.

Midterms: Dates and Locations:
_____   _____
_____   _____

Accredited National Participation - topic/dates: *See page 6 of this application for details*
_____   _____
_____   _____
_____   _____
_____   _____

If not a school or club owner, at whose facility do you teach or manage?
Name: _____ Location _____ School # _____
Name: _____ Location _____ School # _____

School/Club Owner: Licensed facilities you have owned (if extra space is needed, attach additional pages)
#_____ Location _____ Date: from – to _____ Avg. # testing _____
#_____ Location _____ Date: from – to _____ Avg. # testing _____
#_____ Location _____ Date: from – to _____ Avg. # testing _____

Your Junior Instructors who own schools or clubs: (if extra space is needed, attach additional pages)
Name _____ #_____ Location _____
Name _____ #_____ Location _____
Name _____ #_____ Location _____

FOR HQ OFFICE USE ONLY:
Date App Received _____ DVD Received _____ Training Instructor/Senior of Record Approval _____ _____
Pd $_____ Paid Via & date _____ Licensee – Account Information:
Rank _____ Time in Rank _____ Status: ATA _____ WMA _____
Age Req. _____ Numbers: Test/New _____ Testing Results: _____

h/tsh/testing/appsasofsep08/test&midapphighrankmay13.doc

ATA / STF / WTTU International HQ
PO Box 193010, Little Rock, AR 72219
Inst. Dept. Ext. 2268: Fax Number: 866-423-5430

12/23/2013 this sheet supersedes any previously dated or undated material regarding testing requirements. (First adopted 2/9/05)

TESTING REQUIREMENT:
Leadership Points / Accredited National Participation / Titles
(Testing <u>for</u> the rank of 5th Degree <u>and Above</u>)

Leadership Credit points can be obtained through a combination of the following;

Testing numbers	Instruction Seminars (hosted by HQ)
New member numbers	Business Seminars (hosted by HQ)
Tournament judging	Protech Certification/Camp (hosted by HQ)
Regional Testing guest judging	Overseas activities (hosted by HQ)
National Camp participation	Program/Material development (via HQ)

** There IS NO Grandfather clause – individuals will not receive permission to test until the total required leadership credit points for their rank has been achieved.

These credit points should be accumulated throughout the "time-in-rank" requirement;

4th Degree Black Belt = 360 points (90 credits per year for 4 years).
5th Degree Black Belt = 450 points (90 credits per year for 5 years).
6th Degree Black Belt = 540 points (90 credits per year for 6 years).
7th Degree Black Belt = 630 points (90 credits per year for 7 years).
8th Degree Black Belt = 720 points (90 credits per year for 8 years).

I. Leadership Point Accumulation

    A. Numbers (are tabulated from the last full year prior to testing date)

4DB 100 new members or a test number average of	100
5DB 300 new members or a test number average of	300
6DB 1000 new members or a test number average of	1000
7DB 3000 new members or a test number average of	3000
8DB 6000 new members or a test number average of	6000

Meeting 10% of required numbers =	5 Leader points per year time in rank
Meeting 20% of required numbers =	10 Leader points per year time in rank
Meeting 30% of required numbers =	15 Leader points per year time in rank
Meeting 40% of required numbers =	20 Leader points per year time in rank
Meeting 50% of required numbers =	25 Leader points per year time in rank
Meeting 60% of required numbers =	30 Leader points per year time in rank
Meeting 70% of required numbers =	35 Leader points per year time in rank
Meeting 80% of required numbers =	40 Leader points per year time in rank
Meeting 100% of required numbers =	50 Leaders Points per year time in rank

ATA / STF / WTTU International HQ
PO Box 193010, Little Rock, AR 72219
Inst. Dept. Ext. 2268: Fax Number: 866-423-5430

12/23/2013

B. Leadership Credit Points: Tournament Judging or Staff
- 1 Point   Per Ring Judged at Regional's – Max 20 per year
- 2 Points   Per Ring Judged at Nationals – Max 14 per year
- 3 Points   Per Ring Judged at Worlds – Max 12 per year

** Make sure to put your ATA Number on all tournament ring packets next to your name!

C. Leadership Points: Personal Improvement / Leadership Activities
- 15 Points   Leadership Camp
- 15 Points   Protech Camp
- 15 Points   Korea Trips hosted by HQ
- 10 Points   National Instructor Certification Upgrade/Re-cert Camps
- 5 Points   World Conference Topics
- 5 Points   Regional Camps/Seminars - Max 20 points per year
- 5 Points   Instruction Seminars – Max 20 points per year
- 5 Points   Business Seminars - Maximum 20 points per year
- 5 Points   Protech Seminars - Maximum 20 points per year
- 5 Points   MASS Training Seminar – Maximum 10 points per year

D. Leadership Points: Regional Testing Guest Judge
- 5 Points   Guest Judge at a regional test – Max 20 points per year
  ** Make sure to keep your own records of dates and locations!

E. Leadership Points: Contributions to Organization / Community Participation
- 10 Points   Development of new programs/material
- 10 Points   Community Work/Contribution

F. Personal Improvement Seminars (Krav Maga, Leadership, etc.)
At this time points will not be awarded however, these "other" seminars may be taken into consideration by the Grand Master in making his final decision towards approval.

Note 1:   Individuals must achieve their required point total within their "time-in-rank". If they fall short, at the end of their required time in rank minimum, they must wait the extra year or years it takes to reach the required total for their rank.

Note 2:   To test, individuals do not have to acquire points in testing or new member numbers, they can make up the numbers by achieving points in other activities.

ATA / STF / WTTU International HQ
PO Box 193010, Little Rock, AR 72219
Inst. Dept. Ext. 2268: Fax Number: 866-423-5430

12/23/2013

II. Accredited National Training Participation:

All Black Belts age 18 years and up, who attain the rank of 3rd Degree Black Belt through 7th Degree Black Belt as of January 1, 2013 and after, are required to participate in Accredited National Leadership Training Activities.

Accredited National Leadership Training Activities are:
- World Conference (part of World Expo)
- HQ Leadership Camp / Songahm Training Camp
- HQ Protech Camp
- HQ Korea Trips
- Jacksonville Master's Gathering

The amount/number breakdown, by rank, is as follows:
- 3rd Degree -   1
- 4th Degree -   2
- 5th Degree -   5
- 6th Degree -   6
- 7th Degree -   7

III. Testing VS Title consideration

See the Testing Application for requirements needed to receive testing approval. These requirements are different from the Mastership Title process.

There are 3 stages to the Mastership Process.
a. Candidate status is achieved when appropriate rank is awarded.
b. Nominee status is achieved via these initial requirements & official invitation
   i. Numbers – Testing average OR New Members
      - Master Title   200
      - Sr. Master Title   500
      - Ch. Master Title   1000
   ii. OR – National Leadership Training Participation
      - Master Title   9 (combined 4th – 5th degree participation)
      - Sr. Master   6 (6th degree participation)
      - Ch Master   7 (7th degree participation)
   iii. Owners Must
      - Have all in-school testing results up-to-date & paid in full
      - Have all accounts paid in full (ATA/STF/WTTU & WMA)
c. Inductee status is achieved when all nominee application requirements are met.

My Notes on My Road to Master

Leadership Training Applications

The following pages contain additional forms that need to be filled out for entry into the Championship Option of the Leadership Program. Note that the fees are not included in your program cost, so let one of our instructors help you with this - it's your responsibility to make sure this gets sent in.

Application for Kids:

Kids younger than 13 need to fill this form out to be registered nationally in the <u>Championship Option</u> of the Leadership Program. This will allow you to also collect points towards State Champion (and World Champion for Black Belt)! Your points will not be counted until you send this in.

Application for Adults:

Adults (or teens 13 or older) need to fill this form out as well including the "Youth Protection" portion.

STUDENT LEADERSHIP PROGRAM APPLICATION
ATA / WTTU / STF Int. HQ, PO Box 193010, Little Rock, AR 72219
Inst. Fax; Ext. 2265: 866-423-5429, Ext. 2268: 866-423-5430

12/11/2013

_____ No Book
_____ (Jr. Lead) Student Leadership Application: 15 Yrs. Old <u>& Younger</u> – Red/White/Blue Collar
_____ (Leader) Student Leadership Application: 13 Yrs. Old <u>& Up</u> – Red Collar
_____ (Leader Upgrade) Upgrade within Leadership - from Red/White/Blue to Red Collar: Minimum 13 Yrs. Old
____ of ____ # FAMILY MEMBER (applying at the same time or already in program)

ATA/WTTU # _____ New, need ATA # ___ Transfer from Other ATA Schl ____, Owned by _____

Name _____ Male __ Female __ DOB ___/___/___ Age _____ Rank _____
    Family name, if different than **Name** above: _____
Address _____
City/State/Zip _____ County (not country) _____
Home Phone (___) ___-_____ Work Phone (___) ___-_____ Cell Phone (___) ___-_____
E-Mail Address _____ Alternate E-Mail Address _____

ALL APPLICANTS
Applicants will not receive State Champ Points until all appropriate paperwork and fees have been <u>received and processed by ATA HQ</u>.
Applications will not be backdated by ATA HQ as this affects everyone within the organization

YOUTH PROTECTION – <u>13 & Older</u> APPLICANTS must read and sign below
What is Child Abuse?
Generally speaking, child abuse is injury of a child by an adult or older child. It is usually classified as physical abuse, emotional abuse, or sexual abuse. Harm caused by withholding life's necessities-food, clothing, shelter, medical care and education-is called neglect.

What should you do if you suspect that a child is being abused?
Call the proper authorities immediately. If you suspect a child is being abused, you should contact your local child abuse hotline. Generally the telephone number to report child abuse is listed in the white pages under "child abuse". If you suspect a child is in immediate danger, the local police agency should be contacted first. If the suspect is a volunteer, student or instructor of an ATA/STF/WTTU school or club, notify Headquarters AFTER the police have been notified.

How do I know what my reporting responsibilities are?
People are often concerned about being sued for reporting child abuse. You are not required to know for certain that a child has been abused. All that the law requires is that you have a reasonable suspicion and are reporting in "good faith". When this requirement is met, all states provide immunity for child abuse reporters.

Youth Protection policies and procedures:
1. Volunteers, students, and instructors accused of abuse will be placed on ATA suspension until local authorities complete their investigation. Suspension includes no allowance or participation at or near any ATA/STF/WTTU school (including their own, if suspect is an owner), club, or event.
2. If found innocent of all accusations, all privileges will be re-instated. If found guilty all association membership will be revoked!

I understand that as a Student Leader <u>I may not teach class</u> or be in charge of minors without receiving an approved background check.
I signify that I HAVE READ AND UNDERSTAND THE POLICIES LISTED ABOVE AS INDICATED BY checking the appropriate Signature box below

Applicant's signature: _____
If Minor: Signature of Parent or Legal Guardian: _____
Printed name of Parent/Legal Guardian: _____

Licensee Name: _____ Schl. number _____
City/State/Zip _____ Country _____
Phone Number _____

Payment to HQ via: Credit Card ___ EFT ___ Check ___ Do <u>not</u> e-mail or fax if paying by check.. Print app and mail with check.

Credit Card Expire Date _____ Credit Card # _____ (if <u>on file</u> at HQ, supply last 4 digits)
Name on Credit Card _____

ATA HQ USE ONLY: Due: _____ Paid: _____ Paid BG: _____ Pymt Type: _____ Date Received: _____

My Notes on My Road to Master

Supplemental Material

The following pages contain supplemental material.

Beginner Rank Requirements: 1-Steps

You will learn 1-Steps and Sparring Segments during this portion of your training. These are combinations of moves designed to help take your sparring to the next level. These will be done with a partner to develop an appropriate response to an attack. These techniques will prepare you for self-defense in real world situations. Karate kids will only perform the first two 1-steps.

Beginner 1-Step

Rotation A 1-Steps

1-Step Number 1

Attacker:

Step	Technique
1	Step Back with right foot into Sparring Stance, Low Block
2	Responding to Defender Kihap, Right Punch (Face Level)

Defender:

Step	Technique
1	Right Foot Steps, Dodging Back, Left Double Outer Forearm Block
2	#3 Jump Front Kick (with Left Foot)
3	Left Knifehand Strike
4	Right Punch
5	Double Step Back, Left Double Outer Forearm Block - Kihap!

1-Step Number 2

Attacker:

Step	Technique
1	Step Back with right foot into Sparring Stance, Low Block
2	Responding to Defender Kihap, Right Punch (Face Level)

Defender:

Step	Technique
1	Left Foot Steps, Dodging Back, Roght Double Outer Forearm Block
2	#3 Jump Front Kick (with Right Foot)
3	Right Backfist
4	Left Punch
5	Right Punch
6	#1 Round Kick (Right Foot)
7	Double Step Back, Right Double Outer Forearm Block - Kihap!

1-Step Number 3

Attacker:

Step	Technique
1	Step Back with right foot into Sparring Stance, Arm Base
2	Responding to Defender Kihap, Right #2 Side Kick (Low Level)

Defender:

Step	Technique
1	Left Foot Steps back to Middle Stance, Right Low Block
2	Step back with right foot, spin and step forward with left foot, Left Backfist
3	Left Knifehand Strike
4	Step back with left foot
5	Right Round Kick
6	Double Step Back, Right Double Outer Forearm Block - Kihap!

Rev 4.0 - © KarateBuilt L.L.C.

Beginner 1-Step

Rotation B 1-Steps

1-Step Number 1

Attacker:

Step	Technique
1	Step Back with right foot into Sparring Stance, Low Block
2	Responding to Defender Kihap, Right Punch (Face Level)

Defender:

Step	Technique
1	Right Foot Steps, Dodging Back, Left Double Outer Forearm Block
2	Left Backfist
3	Right Punch
4	Step Back Right Round Kick
5	Step Back Right Double Outer Forearm Block - Kihap!

1-Step Number 2

Attacker:

Step	Technique
1	Step Back with right foot into Sparring Stance, Low Block
2	Responding to Defender Kihap, Right Punch (Face Level)

Defender:

Step	Technique
1	Left Foot Steps, Dodging Back, Roght Double Outer Forearm Block
2	Right Round Kick
3	Left Backfist
4	Step Back, Left Side Kick
5	Double Step Back, LeftDouble Outer Forearm Block - Kihap!

1-Step Number 3

Attacker:

Step	Technique
1	Step Back with right foot into Sparring Stance, Arm Base
2	Responding to Defender Kihap, Right #2 Round Kick (Mid/High Level)

Defender:

Step	Technique
1	Right Foot Steps, Dodging Back, Left Double Outer Forearm Block (if round kick is low you may execute a Low Block instead)
2	Right Punch
3	Left Punch
4	#1 Left Side Kick
5	Double Step Back, Left Double Outer Forearm Block - Kihap!

Beginner 1-Step

Rotation C 1-Steps

1-Step Number 1

Attacker:

Step	Technique
1	Step Back with right foot into Sparring Stance, Low Block
2	Responding to Defender Kihap, Right Punch (Face Level)

Defender:

Step	Technique
1	Right Foot Steps Back, High Block
2	Right Punch (mid)
3	Left Punch (mid)
4	Right Punch (high)
5	Double Step Back, Left Low Block - Kihap!

1-Step Number 2

Attacker:

Step	Technique
1	Step Back with right foot into Sparring Stance, Low Block
2	Responding to Defender Kihap, Right Punch (Face Level)

Defender:

Step	Technique
1	Left Foot Steps Back To Middle Stance, Right Inner Forearm Block
2	#1 Side Kick (with Right Foot)
3	Right Knifehand Strike
4	Right Leg Steps Back to Front Stance, Left Low Block - Kihap!

1-Step Number 3

Attacker:

Step	Technique
1	Step Back with right foot into Sparring Stance, Arm Base
2	Responding to Defender Kihap, Right #2 Front Kick (Mid Level)

Defender:

Step	Technique
1	Right Foot Steps back to Front Stance, Left Low Block
2	#1 Front Kick (with Left Foot)
3	Right Punch (mid)
4	Left Punch
5	Double Step Back, Left Low Block

Rev 4.0 - © KarateBuilt L.L.C.

Intermediate Rank Requirements:
1-Steps and Sparring Segments

You will learn 1-Steps and Sparring Segments during this portion of your training. These are combinations of moves designed to help take your sparring to the next level. Sometimes these are done with a partner to develop an appropriate response to an attack. These techniques will help improve your sparring and prepare you for real world situations.

Intermediate Segments

Rotation A - Sparring Segments
Note that these may be done individually or in order in a line as combinations separated by a Kihap

Sparring Segment Number 1
Start in Left Sparring Stance

Move	Technique
1	Left Outer Forearm Block
2	Left Hook Kick
3	Right Reverse Punch
4	#2 Jump Round Kick
5	Right Knifehand Strike (to neck)
6	Left Ridgehand Strike (to neck)

Sparring Segment Number 2
Start in Right Sparring Stance

Move	Technique
1	#1 Jump Round Kick
2	Left Low Block
3	Left Round Kick
4	Left Backfist (high)
5	Right Punch (mid)
6	Left Punch (high)
7	Right Foot Steps Forward, Reverse Hook / Round Kick

Sparring Segment Number 3
Start in Left Sparring Stance

Move	Technique
1	#4 Hook Kick (step with left, kick with right)
2	Right Outer Forearm Block
3	Left Reverse Punch (high)
4	Left Low Block
5	Left Outer Forearm Block
6	#2 Jump Front Kick

Rev 4.0 - © KarateBuilt L.L.C.

Intermediate 1-Steps

Rotation B - 1-Steps

1-Step Number 1

Attacker:

Step	Technique
1	Step Back with right foot into Sparring Stance, Advanced Arm Base
2	Responding to Defender Kihap, Step Forward, Right Punch

Defender:

Step	Technique
1	Left Foot Steps back to Middle Stance
2	Double Side Kick
3	Left Reverse Outer Crescent
4	Left Backfist (High Section)
5	Right Punch (Mid Section)
6	Left Round Kick, Finish Step Back to Advanced Arm Base - **Ki-hap!**

1-Step Number 2

Attacker:

Step	Technique
1	Step Back with right foot into Sparring Stance, Advanced Arm Base
2	Responding to Defender Kihap, Step Forward, Right Punch

Defender:

Step	Technique
1	Dodge to Left, Right Spearhand
2	Left Double Round Kick
3	Right Reverse Outer Crescent
4	Left Side Kick, Finish Step Back to Advanced Arm Base - **Ki-hap!**

1-Step Number 3

Attacker:

Step	Technique
1	Step Back with right foot into Sparring Stance, Advanced Arm Base
2	Responding to Defender Kihap, #3 Left Jump Side Kick

Defender:

Step	Technique
1	Dodge to Right, Double Outer Forearm Block
2	Right Punch (Mid Section), Left Punch (High Section)
3	Right Ridgehand (High Section), Left Ridgehand (Mid Section)
4	Left Knifehand Strike (High Section)
5	Step back, #3 Jump Side Kick, Finish Step Back to Advanced Arm Base

Intermediate 1-Steps

Rotation C - 1-Steps

1-Step Number 1
Attacker:

Step	Technique
1	Step Back with right foot into Sparring Stance, Advanced Arm Base
2	Responding to Defender Kihap, Step Forward, Right Punch

Defender:

Step	Technique
1	Dodge Right, Arm Base
2	#1 Left Front Kick
3	Left Backfist (High)
4	#1 Left Side Kick
5	Right Reverse Side Kick, Land in Front, Arm Base - **Ki-hap!**

1-Step Number 2
Attacker:

Step	Technique
1	Step Back with right foot into Sparring Stance, Advanced Arm Base
2	Responding to Defender Kihap, Step Forward, Right Punch

Defender:

Step	Technique
1	Step Back, Right Inner Crescent
2	Left Reverse Side Kick
3	Right Punch
4	Left Punch,
5	#2 Right Jump Front Kick, Land in Front, Arm Base - **Ki-hap!**

1-Step Number 3
Attacker:

Step	Technique
1	Step Back with right foot into Sparring Stance, Advanced Arm Base
2	Responding to Defender Kihap, Right reverse side kick (Middle)

Defender:

Step	Technique
1	Left Foot Steps to Left, Evade Kick, Right low block
2	Right outer crescent kick
3	Left inner crescent kick
4	Left outer crescent kick
5	Right Punch (High)
6	Right round kick, Land in Front, Arm Base - **Ki-hap!**

Rev 4.0 - © KarateBuilt L.L.C.

Advanced Rank Requirements:
Sparring Segments

Sparring Segments are combinations of moves designed to help take your sparring to the next level. These are not typically done with a partner because you are now past the stimulus/response stage of training (responding to a simple punch or kick). If you work hard on these moves, you will excel at sparring. <u>Note that only adults are required to perform this at graduation</u>.

Sparring Segments - A

Sparring Segment Number 1
Step Back With Left Foot

Move	Technique	R/L
1	Backfist	Right
2	Reverse Punch	Left
3	Step Reverse Punch	Right
4	#2 Jump Side Kick	Right
5	Spin Heel Kick	Left
6	#3 Jump Hook Kick	Right
7	Reverse Punch	Left

Sparring Segment Number 2
Step Back With Left Foot

Move	Technique	R/L
1	Backfist	Right
2	Double Step	
3	Reverse Punch	Left
3	Step Jump Reverse Side Kick	Right
4	Reverse Punch	Left

Sparring Segment Number 3
Step Back With Left Foot

Move	Technique	R/L
1	Backfist	Right
2	#3 Jump Hook Kick	Right
3	Step Front Punch	Left
4	Jump Reverse Inner Crescent Kick	Left
5	Reverse Hook Kick, Round Kick Combination	Right
6	Reverse Punch	Left

Rev 4.0 - © KarateBuilt L.L.C.

MC Curriculum - Sparring Segments

Sparring Segments - B

Sparring Segment Number 1
Step Back With Right Foot

Move	Technique	R/L
1	Front Punch	Left
2	Backfist	Left
3	Reverse Punch	Right
4	Step Reverse Ridgehand	Left
5	#2 Twist Kick	Left
6	Jump Spin Heel Kick	Right
7	Sliding Side Kick & Round Kick Combination	Left
8	Reverse Punch	Right

Sparring Segment Number 2
Step Back With Right Foot

Move	Technique	R/L
1	Backfist	Left
2	Double Step, Reverse Punch	Right
3	Step Backfist	Right
4	Reverse Punch	Left
5	360° Jump Side Kick	Right
6	Reverse Punch	Left

Sparring Segment Number 3
Step Back With Right Foot

Move	Technique	R/L
1	Fake Switch Back, 180° Turn	
2	Double Switch	
3	#3 Axe Kick	Right
4	Reverse Punch	Left
5	#2 Round Kick	Left
6	Jump Spin Heel Kick	Right
7	Jump Reverse Side Kick	Right

Sparring Segments - C

Sparring Segment Number 1
Step Back With Right Foot

Move	Technique	R/L
1	Outer Crescent	Left
2	Outer Forearm Block	Right
3	Punch	Left
4	Reverse Punch	Right
5	Low Block	Left
6	Jump Spin Outer Crescent	Right
7	Backfist (mid)	Left
8	Punch (high)	Right
9	Backfist (high)	Right
10	Punch (mid) - **Kihap**	Left

Sparring Segment Number 2
Step Back With Right Foot

Move	Technique	R/L
1	#2 Side Kick	Right
2	Jump Spin Outer Crescent	Left
3	Punch	Right
4	Reverse Punch	Left
5	Palm Heel	Right
6	#3 Jump Outer Crescent	Right

Sparring Segment Number 3
Step Back With Left Foot

Move	Technique	R/L
1	Punch, Knifehand Strike	Right
2	Spin Backfist, Spin Hook Kick	Left
3	#1 Round Kick, Hook Kick	Right
4	Reverse Side Kick	Left
5	#3 Jump Side Kick	Left

Rev 4.0 - © KarateBuilt L.L.C.